Teach Me Series:

How to Run
Beginners and Next Steps

by
Maxine Morrison

TEACH ME: How to Run

Table of Contents

Dedication

Acknowledgement

Foreword by Brent Fougner

Introduction	1
Chapter 1 – Preparation and Motivation	3
Chapter 2 – Training Guide	11
Chapter 3 – Injury Prevention	37
Chapter 4 – Stretching and Flexibility	47
Chapter 5 – Nutrition and Hydration	59
Chapter 6 – Rest and Recovery	67
Chapter 7 – Core Stability	81
Chapter 8 – Weight Training	91
Chapter 9 – Race Day Preparations	107
Glossary of Terms	113
Bibliography	117

TEACH ME: How to Run

Books in the **How to Run** Series soon to be published:

Teach me: How to Run a 10K Faster
Teach Me: How to Run from 10K to Marathon
Teach Me: Core Stability and Flexibility
Teach Me: Weight Training

For details about the above books visit our website
www.redboxbooks.org

If you have any questions with reference to this How to Run book please e-mail: **maxine@redboxbooks.org**

Dedication

I would like to dedicate this book to my parents Ray and Vivienne Jamieson.

They have always supported me and encouraged me to be the best I can.

I know it must have been a huge disappointment to them and when I told them I was going to Canada, but they were happy for me and wished me well.

I couldn't have done any of this without them and want to Thank them and tell them how much I Love You both.

Maxine xox

Acknowledgement

I would like to acknowledge two people who have helped me with this book.

Firstly, my friend and Mentor **Istvan Balyi**.

I met Istvan in Loughborough, England in 2002. He gave a lecture on Long Term Athlete Development and I managed to talk to him afterwards for no more than 5 minutes. From that conversation, I decided to travel to Canada to complete my Level 4 Coaching Diploma in Middle Distance Running!

Istvan is acknowledged as the worldwide expert in Long Term Athlete Development and the periodization of training plans. He is currently employed by many sports helping to re-develop their long-term high performance programs.

He has always been very supportive and I would like him to know how much I have appreciated all his help and advice.

Secondly, **Sheryl Mearns** at National Coaching Institute.

She has been a constant friend and support from the first day I arrived, and still is today. Thank you for helping me in so many ways, and, to become Canadian!

Maxine

Foreword

It is often the case that running books are written by long time runners or coaches who don't remember how hard it was to learn how to run!

This book captures the concept of how hard it is for the beginner, to start running, who has never run before. In fact this book has been written for adult runners by an adult runner, who herself only started running in 2003.

The easy to read charts and comprehensive information along with motivational tips, nutrition ideas and injury prevention plan prepares the reader for a gradual and consistent progression from walker to runner!

I met Maxine in 2003 when she was a student at the National Coaching Institute located at the University of Victoria. Maxine having an extensive background in the education field wanted to expand her knowledge into coaching. She found herself in an environment of runners from Varsity athletes to Olympians all focused and dedicated to running. Even the elite coaches she worked with were runners!

It wasn't long before this mom was lacing up the training shoes and hitting the trails. She got advice from the coaches and the athletes but must have realized at some point that to start running for the first time is so different to competitive running.

Her background in child development probably convinced her that a gradual progression from basic movement (walking) to full running was required. Now she has taken all this knowledge and experience and written this very useful book. Good Luck!…………..

Brent Fougner BA Ed.
Head Coach - Cross country/Track
University of Victoria.
Director
Pacific Sport
National Athletics Training Centre

TEACH ME: How to Run

About the Author

I decided to travel to Canada to complete my Level 4 Coaching Diploma as I wanted to increase my knowledge of coaching and also to work with the Middle Distance Canadian National Team Elites. As it turns out; I found I enjoy teaching beginners much more!

Maxine Morrison

I have been involved with exercise in some way for many years. I am a qualified Pilates and Aerobic Instructor and worked in a gym for 10 years before I decided to become a Coach. I got involved as a parent coach and found I loved it so much I decided to take the courses to become a qualified coach. This led me to that fateful day when I attended a lecture in Loughborough as I started my Level 3 coaching course. Istvan was talking about Long Term Athlete Development and how it could improve the coaching of adults and children. We talked; he gave me his card and told me to look on-line at the coaching course in Canada! I moved to Canada in 2003 and it took me 6 weeks to fall in love with Victoria and the people.

Since completing my Level 4 Diploma in Middle Distance Running, I have coached all ages but mostly adult beginners. I have been asked many times which book I would recommend for beginners. I couldn't find one, so I wrote it myself - I hope you find it useful & easy to read.
It is full of information about how to get started and why we coaches ask you to stretch, warm up, cool down and eat properly!

Have fun running; it does get easier, as long as you stick with it.

The hardest part is starting - the rest is all downhill! ☺

Trust me, I'm a Coach!!

TEACH ME: How to Run

Chapter 1 - Preparation and Motivation

Information to know before starting
Motivational tools to keep you at it
Tips and hints about clothing and footwear
Items to prepare
What to do if you miss a week or 2 weeks training
Goal Setting
Skin Care!

Much as I would like you to love running straight away, it is not for everyone! But it can be and with a little preparation, I can ease you into it as opposed to crashing!! This book is here to help.

One of the most important lessons to learn from the start is:

More is not necessarily better!!

Slow consistent progression is the way to prevent injuries, improve your overall health and fitness along with maintaining steady weight loss.

Information to know before starting

Before you start to run, it would be advisable to check with your physician especially if you have never exercised in the past. In some cases, a walking program might be more suitable. On the other hand, if you have been exercising in another sport or haven't run for a while but are fairly healthy and would like to try running, then this is the book for you.

Motivation tools to keep you at it

What keeps you Motivated? – YOU!

There are many ways you can motivate yourself. For me I used to like to run on my own, but now I am converted to running with a group. After organising my clinics and talking to the runners as we go out on our training runs, it is great to have someone to talk to and the time whizzes by!

Run with a buddy! It is much harder to sleep in or get out of training when someone is coming to meet you and banging on your door. If you find you can't motivate yourself very well, get someone to run with.

Join a running group. Many of the shoe stores have running groups that meet once a week and usually you can join one for free. You don't have to be a good runner as they should have all abilities with different groups for beginners to advanced.

Join a training clinic. These generally meet once a week and teach you the basics of how to run, provide you with a training plan and it includes a training run each week. A great way to meet like minded people and knowing you have to be there each week gets you out.

Tips and hints about clothing

Let's start with clothing. Most people get their cotton tee shirt; sweatshirt top and jogging pants out and off they go. This is great to start with but the problem with sweatshirt material is once you start to sweat it holds in the water which apart from becoming heavy adding to the weight you are already carrying, it lets the wind whistle through! This is great on a hot day when you are unlikely to be wearing that anyway, but on a windy day you can easily get a chill. Start with this for the first and second week and then invest in some specially designed running clothing. You don't have to spend a lot but remember this will last you a long time and save you a lot of unnecessary discomfort!

You will need a long or short sleeved **shirt** made of the type of material that lets the sweat out but keeps the heat in. **Long pants** of the running type - not yoga pants! I like to layer up because you can always take off. If you are out and don't have anything to put on and it is gets cold tough luck! It is always good to have a **waterproof jacket**. At the end of your run, as you do your cool down, you will feel cold and it is much better to have something to put on that will prevent the cold wind giving you a chill.

Next come the accessories!

Hats are good if you don't like cold ears and in the summer are prefect for keeping the sun out of your eyes. Even when you are wearing sunglasses the sun can get in, so a hat or visor does the trick.
Speaking of **glasses** I find I can't run in the sun without them as I get a headache. Try and get them close to the eyes and as long as they are UV protected you don't need to spend too much.
Scarves again are a personal choice.
If you are running at night it is always good to have a light reflective **band/sash** on your jacket or top.
A **light** is always handy at night, just in case.
Water bottle - should you carry one or not? I personally find the added weight a problem and it always bumps up and down. Some runners can't run without one. I find it is better to have a drink when I finish my run, and

drink it as I cool down or when I have stopped.
Backpack - these would usually be for the long distance runner doing a 20Km run, out for an hour or two. For the beginner, I would recommend that you don't need to bother.
Lastly, **socks**, before I move onto shoes. These can be the worst or best. If you have a pair or socks that are rubbing as you run, STOP and change them or don't run. For those of you that have had a blister on your foot and then tried to run the next day - you know how much it hurts!! You can get socks that have a double layer of material which are supposed to stop you getting blisters. I have found them to be excellent and worth the extra money.

Footwear

Shoes are the most important part of your running equipment and can be the best investment. As I said before, spend as much as you can on shoes. The impact on your body as your feet hit the ground, when you run, is 7 times your body weight. The more shock absorption you can get the better. Go to a specialist shoe store when buying running shoes and DON'T buy cheap shoes. The best bargains can be found at the end of the season when the designs are changing. You can get the last year's model at great discounts! The shoe store should check your foot for alignment and determine if your foot pronates or supernates. If they don't tell you about this - go to another store and talk to a trained shoe fitter. Some people wear orthotics. The shoes should have inserts that can be taken out for them to go in instead. (Orthotics`s are something that you might want to consider in the future as they re-align the foot and help correct your posture.) Always run in the running shoes before you buy them and don't feel embarrassed about running around the store. Try them for 5—10 minutes and then you will know. They should be light weight and fit like a glove!!

Items to prepare for running

I have covered all the clothing items but what else do you need.
- Firstly, map out your route. This may seem obvious but it is always good to know where you are going and how long it takes to get there.
- Always carry some money – a quarter is good so you can use the telephone, if you get lost or too tired.
- It is also recommended that you carry ID just in case of any emergency or mishap.

What if I miss some training runs?

What if you have to miss a run? Don't worry about missing a run during the week as long as you do the other training runs. If you miss 2 of the 3 runs, recommended for the week, you will find it a little harder to move on but not impossible!

If you miss 1 week of runs, stay on the week that you got to, then repeat.

If you miss 2 weeks of runs, I would recommend going back to a place where you feel comfortable starting from again, this doesn't have to be at the beginning, it could be back a week or two.

What are your Goals?

Why are you running?

This is a great time to set yourself a goal and think about what it is, you are trying to achieve.
You can have whatever goal you want and don't be influenced by other people and their goals. Many of my participants ask me what should be their goal. It could be a race, a time, a distance - whatever you want.

Many runners want to start by competing in a race, and this can be a great way to begin. Choose a short race and see how you like it. Try to pick a race without too many participants, so you can experience the excitement but not the crush!
If you enjoy it, you can go on to do longer races.

What if you don't want to do races? I am not a great race runner. I don't like the crowds and don't get motivated by people watching me. Your goal could be a time of how long you want to run, a distance you want to run or a speed that you would like to get to. You might want to run three times a week for 20mins, twice a week for 30mins or a 10K every weekend. These are great goals and one of my goals!

What if your goal it isn't for running but for weight loss, fitness level or for health reasons? Running is the fastest way to get fit and lose weight. It is easy to do and you don't have any costly gym or membership costs.

For weight loss - I would suggest three times a week building up to 30mins per run. The weight loss will be more effective if you combine it with a good diet. I talk about Nutrition and Hydration in Chapter 5.

For general fitness and health - the general rule is to exercise for 20mins each day. If you run three times a week for 30mins and a longer run at the weekends, this would cover it.

Skin Care

Have you noticed that many seasoned runners seem to have a honed body but an ancient face!! This came about because the runners wouldn't wear sunscreen. When they started to sweat, the sunscreen used to drip into the eyes and was extremely painful! Nowadays the manufacturing companies make sunscreen that does not run and is made especially for runners.
Sun damage along with the effects of the wind, cold and dryness all contribute to skin damage. A spring day in Victoria can cause the same damage as a sunny day in Florida as 80% of the suns rays can get through clouds plus most individuals don't think to wear sunscreen if it is not extremely hot!
Skin Cancer is becoming more and more frequently reported, due to an increase in outdoor activities and depletion of the ozone layer.

What to do
- Always wear sunscreen year round. Apply 15mins before a run.
- Choose the highest sun factor or total sun block.
- Try to avoid mid-day running.
- In the summer wear a tee shirt and hat or visor. Remember if you can see through the tee shirt the sun can get through, so wear sun screen on all exposed parts.
- Moisturize and condition the skin, even for men, after a run.

TEACH ME: How to Run

Chapter 2 – Training Guide

Comprehensive training guide for the total beginner
How to increase your running to 10K

The following guide can be used for beginners and re-starters!
It is very easy to follow and you will find if you stick to the program and complete the suggested runs during the week you will progress through the program with ease.

The first week will be hard! Please persevere!!

Once you have made it through the first week, each additional week gets a little easier and the next thing you know you will be running for 10mins.

TEACH ME: How to Run

BEGINNERS TRAINING

Always remember to start with a warm up of a brisk walk for 10 minutes. Then mobilize the joints by bending at the wrists, swinging the arms, lifting and circling the shoulders, couple of kick backs, high knees and lastly the cross over walk! When you have finished, walk for 10 minutes to cool down. There are 3 training sessions per week.

WEEK 1

Training Session 1 - 20mins

Run 30 seconds, Walk 4 ½ minutes.   Do this 4 times.

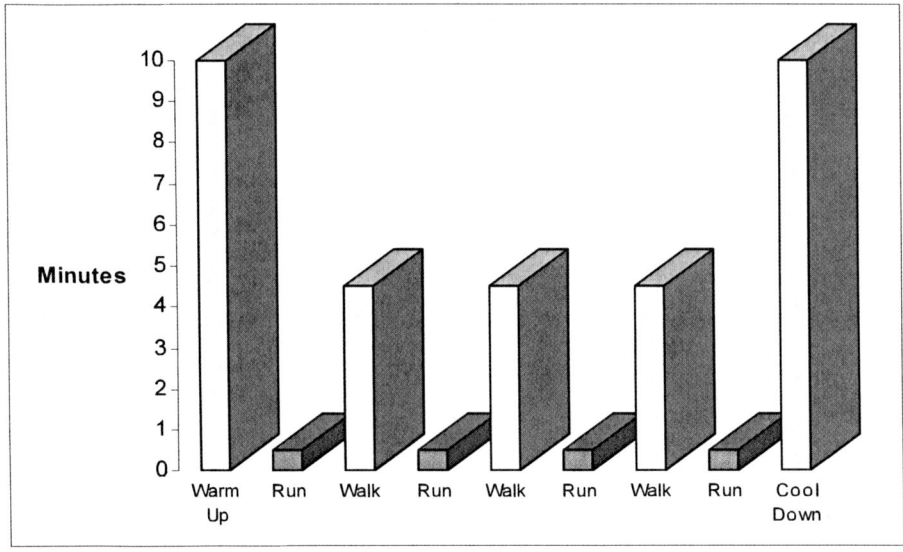

Training Session 2 - 20mins

Run 30 seconds, Walk 4 ½ minutes.   Do this 4 times.

Training Session 3 - 20mins

Run 30 seconds, Walk 4 ½ minutes.   Do this 4 times.

WEEK 2

Well, week one wasn't so bad?
This week we are going to increase the running time a little and think about your arms. Are they crossing in front of the body? If so, try and run with them by your sides and imagine holding some chips in your fore finger and thumb. This helps you from clenching your fists. Drive forward with the arms. Training Session 2 changes this week.
Don't forget to Warm up and Cool down

Training Session 1 - 20mins
Run 45 seconds, Walk 4 minutes and 15 seconds.   Do this 4 times.

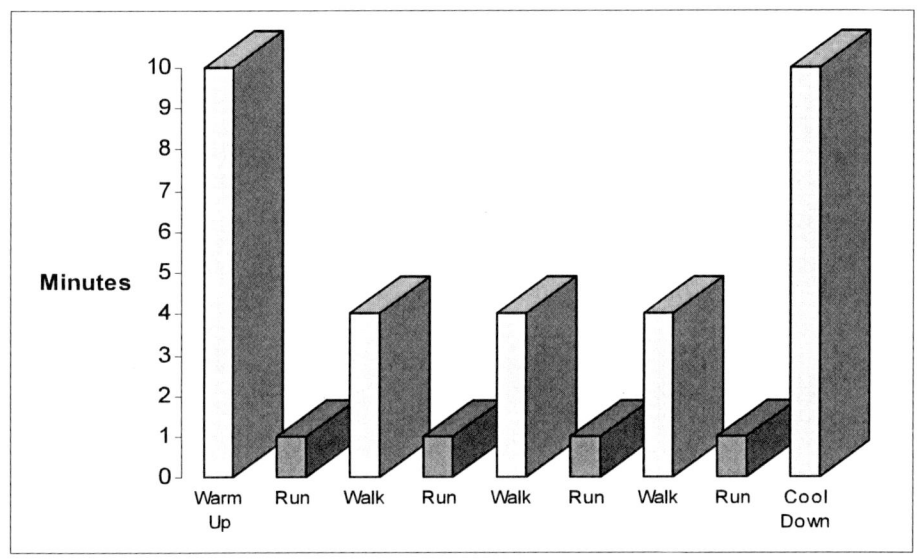

Training Session 2 - 20mins
Run 1 minute, Walk 4 minutes.   Do this 4 times.

Notice the change here

Training Session 3 - 20mins
Run 1 minute, Walk 4 minutes.   Do this 4 times.

WEEK 3

So here we are at week 3.

If you have made it here it is time to buy those shoes and maybe invest in some proper running gear. This week, I would like you to concentrate on your breathing. Breathe in through the nose for 2 seconds and out of the mouth for 2 seconds. Try not to pant.

10 minutes Warm up and Cool down.

Training Session 1 - 20mins
Run 1 minute 30 seconds, Walk 3 minutes 30 seconds. Do this 4 times.

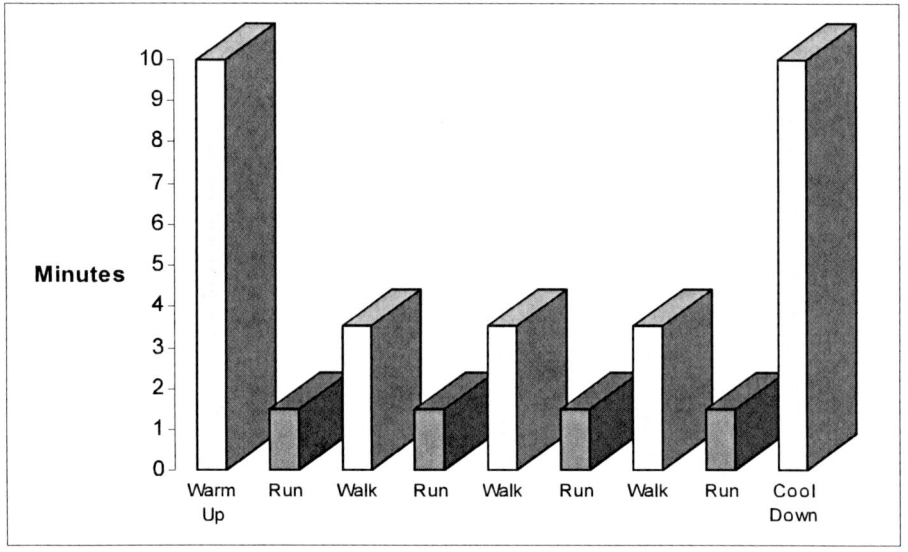

Training Session 2 - 20mins
Run 1 minute 30 seconds, Walk 3 minutes 30 seconds. Do this 4 times.

Training Session 3 - 20mins
Run 1 minute 30 seconds, Walk 3 minutes 30 seconds. Do this 4 times.

CHAPTER 2: Training Guide

WEEK 4

This week we are going to think about Injury Prevention. Read Chapter 3 on Injury Prevention so you will be aware of how NOT to get injured.
Prevention is so much better than treatment!
It is getting a little harder each week but as long as you complete each training session you won't find it too hard!
Don't forget to Warm up and Cool down

Training Session 1 - 20mins
Run 2 minutes, Walk 3 minutes.   Do this 4 times.

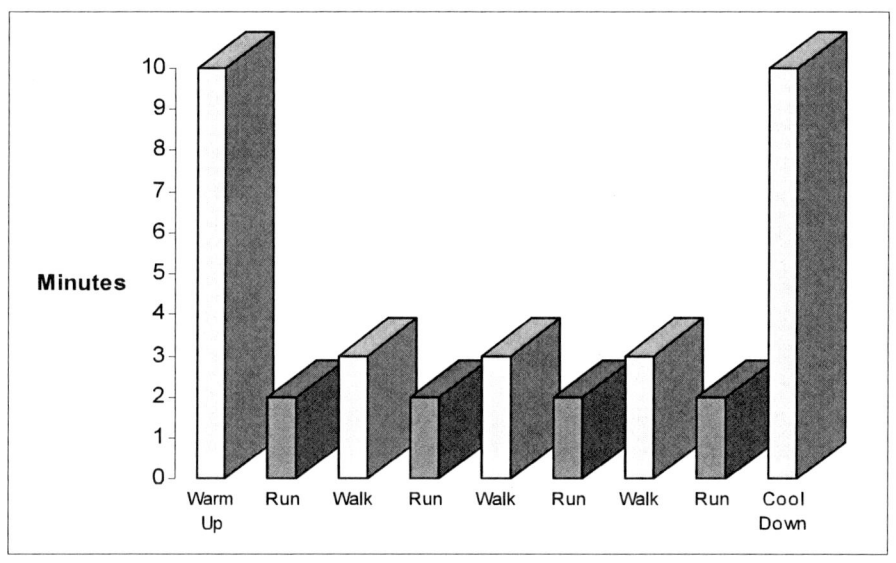

Training Session 2 - 20mins
Run 2 minutes, Walk 3 minutes.   Do this 4 times.

Training Session 3 - 25mins
Run 2 minutes, Walk 3 minutes.   <u>Do this 5 times.</u>   ← *Notice the change here*

WEEK 5

This is the week you might start to think - *Why am I doing this?!!*
Because you are conscious of your health and fitness!
If you have made it so far, it only gets easier from now on. If you are beginning to doubt yourself, now is the time to join a group or get a running buddy. Meet like-minded people to keep yourself motivated.
10 minutes Warm up and Cool down.

Training Session 1 - 20mins
Run 2 minute 30 seconds, Walk 2 minutes 30 seconds. Do this 4 times.

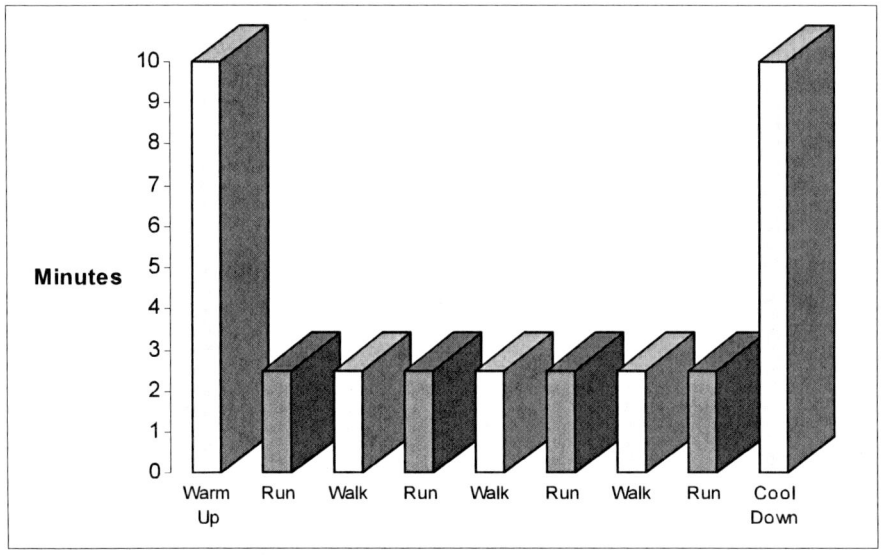

Training Session 2 - 20mins
Run 2 minute 30 seconds, Walk 2 minutes 30 seconds. Do this 4 times.

Training Session 3 - 25mins
Run 2 minute 30 seconds, Walk 2 minutes 30 seconds. Do this 5 times.

CHAPTER 2: Training Guide

WEEK 6

This week we are going to think about your stretching and flexibility. Read Chapter 4 and try to add stretching into your routine. Don't stretch before running as this has been proven to cause injury as the muscles are cold and inflexible. Mobilize the joints first and then run. Stretching really should be done separately from training. If this is not possible, stretch after your run! Warm up and Cool down.

Training Session 1 - 20mins
Run 3 minutes, Walk 2 minutes.   Do this 4 times.

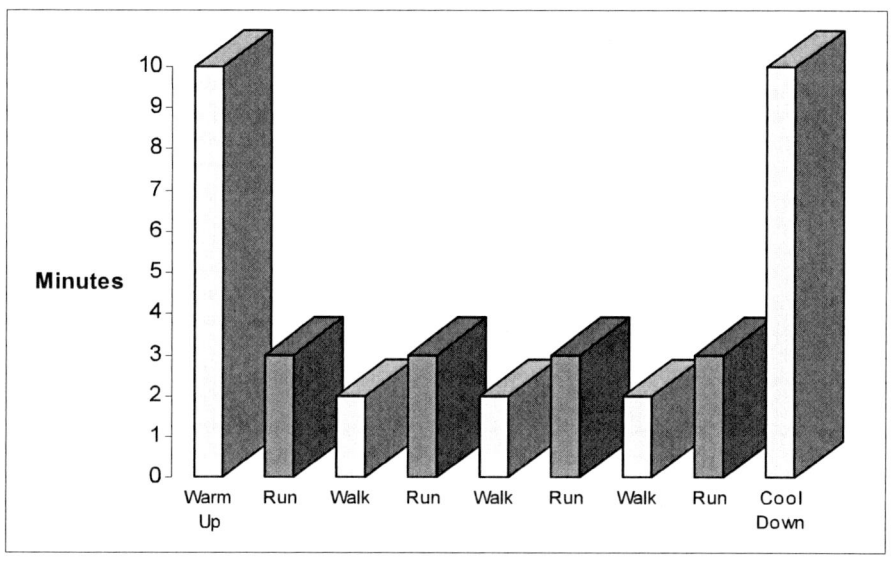

Training Session 2 - 20mins
Run 3 minutes, Walk 2 minutes.   Do this 4 times.

Training Session 3 - 25mins
Run 3 minutes, Walk 2 minutes.   <u>Do this 5 times</u>.

TEACH ME: How to Run

WEEK 7

This week, I would like you to think about your Nutrition and Hydration. If you have not considered this an issue and have been eating the same foods, now is the time to read Chapter 5 on Nutrition and think about your protein intake. Are you getting enough now you are running 3 times a week? Try the protein shake and see if it helps. Water; are you drinking enough?!
10 minutes Warm up and Cool down.

Training Session 1 - 20mins
Run 3 minutes 30 seconds, Walk 1 minute 30 seconds. Do this 4 times.

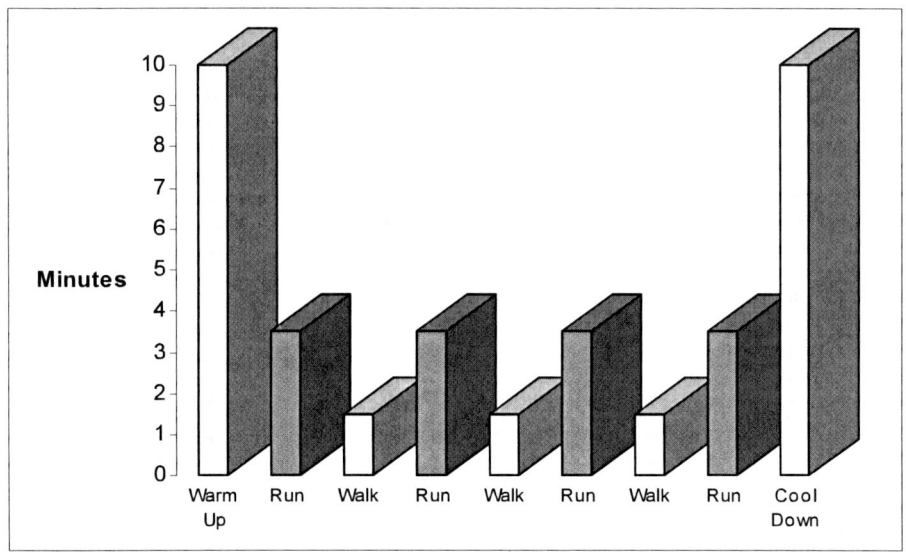

Training Session 2 - 20mins
Run 3 minutes 30 seconds, Walk 1 minute 30 seconds. Do this 4 times.

Training Session 3 - 25mins
Run 3 minutes 30 seconds, Walk 1 minute 30 seconds. <u>Do this 5 times</u>.

CHAPTER 2: Training Guide

WEEK 8

When you are running this week, I would like you to focus on your body. You need to be able tune into it, so you can understand the process of adaptation (how your body is adapting to the exercise). You will then be able to detect any warning signs that could be an indicator of a potential injury. Don't forget to Warm up and Cool down

Training Session 1 - 20mins
Run 4 minutes, Walk 1 minutes.   Do this 4 times.

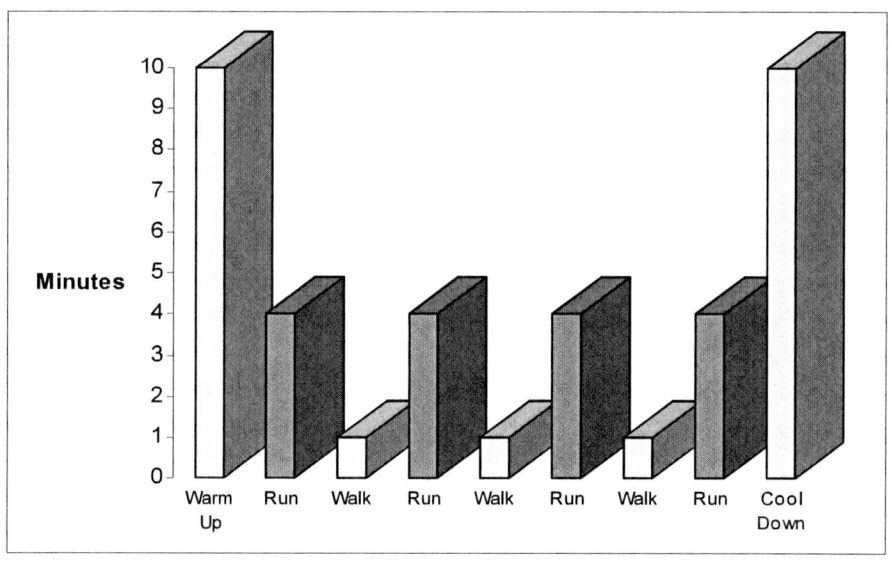

Training Session 2 - 20mins
Run 4 minutes, Walk 1 minutes.   Do this 4 times.

Training Session 3 - 25mins
Run 4 minutes, Walk 1 minutes.   Do this 5 times.

TEACH ME: How to Run

WEEK 9

Are you feeling tired? Are you thinking about your Rest and Recovery? This is a very important week to read Chapter 6 and implement some of the suggestions. The running time is gradually increasing and you will need to be fully rested at the start of each run. Try to get some 'me time' and passive rest. You might consider a massage or trying to reduce your stress by implementing some of the visualising techniques.
10 minutes Warm up and Cool down.

Training Session 1 - 24mins
Run 5 minutes, Walk 1 minute. Do this 4 times.

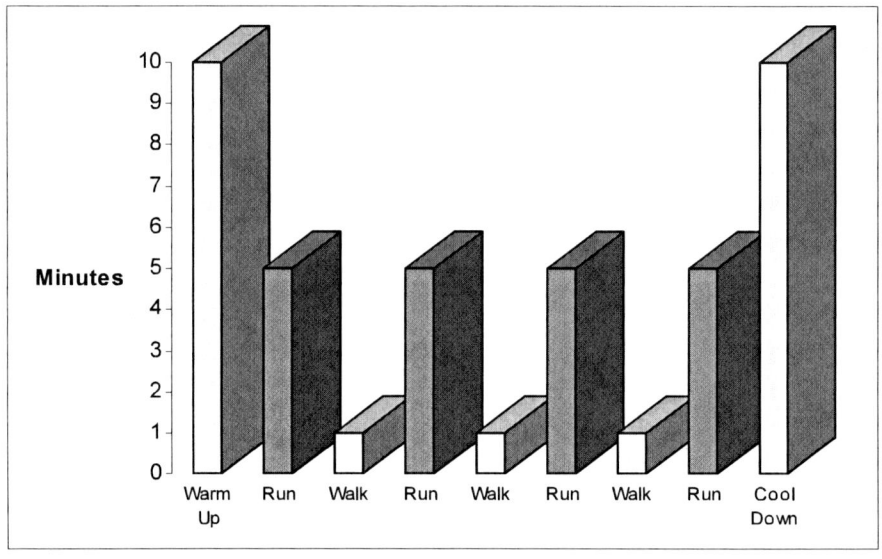

Training Session 2 - 24mins
Run 5 minutes, Walk 1 minute. Do this 4 times.

Training Session 3 - 28mins
Run 6 minutes, Walk 1 minute. Do this 4 times.   ← *Notice the change here*

CHAPTER 2: Training Guide

WEEK 10

Your focus this week is Core Stability. Core Stability is essential for all sport performances as it provides the foundation for all movement. As you run, try to stand up tall and don't bend over at your middle. Imagine wearing a belt just around your hips and tighten those muscles for as long as you can while you are running. You might consider signing up for Pilates classes.
Don't forget to Warm up and Cool down

Training Session 1 - 28mins
Run 6 minutes, Walk 1 minutes. Do this 4 times.

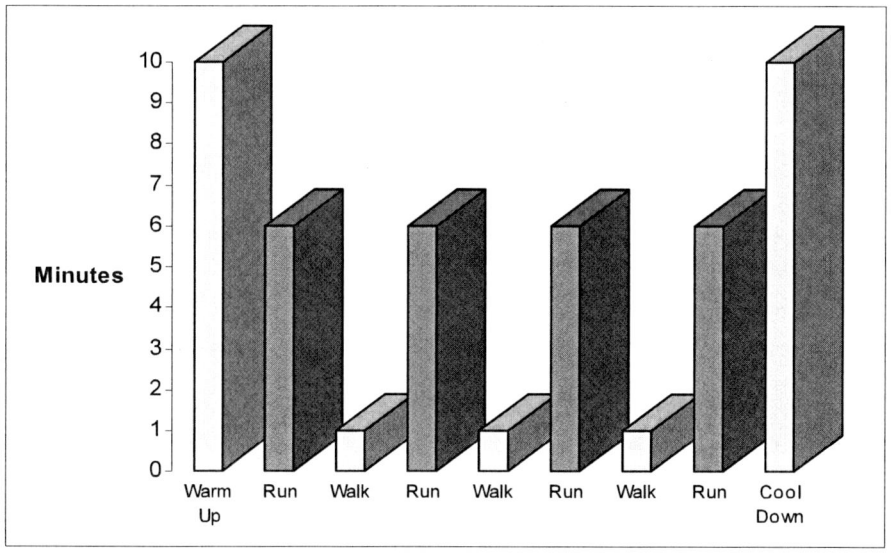

Training Session 2 - 32mins
Run 7 minutes, Walk 1 minutes. Do this 4 times.

Training Session 3 - 32mins
Run 7 minutes, Walk 1 minutes. Do this 4 times.

TEACH ME: How to Run

WEEK 11

Have you thought about weight training? Time to read Chapter 7 on Weight Training. There you will find information on the muscle groups and I have detailed some sport specific exercises for the runner. Stronger muscles will not only make you run faster and longer, but will also burn more calories! 10 minutes Warm up and Cool down.

Training Session 1 - 36mins
Run 8 minutes, Walk 1 minute.   Do this 4 times.

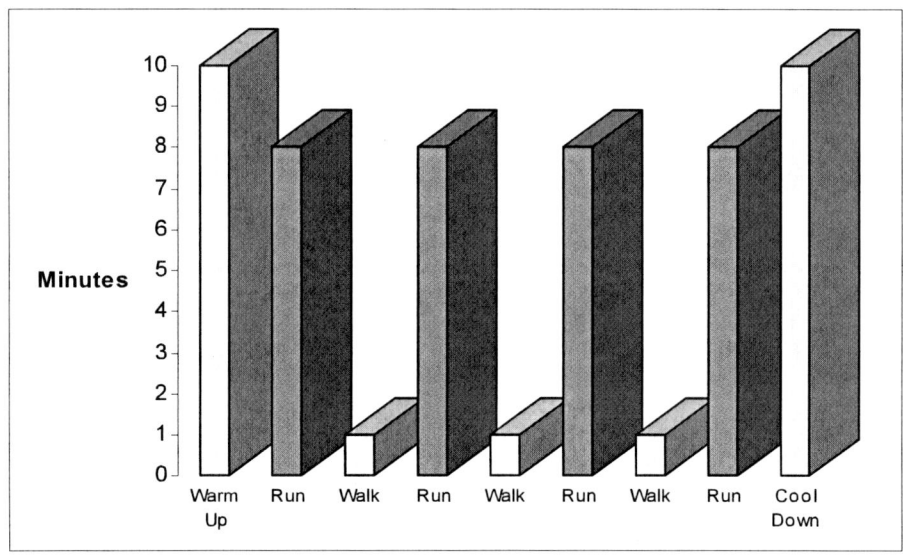

Training Session 2 - 36mins
Run 8 minutes, Walk 1 minute.   Do this 4 times.

Training Session 3 - 40mins
Run 9 minutes, Walk 1 minute.   Do this 4 times.

CHAPTER 2: Training Guide

WEEK 12

So you made it here! This is just the beginning, not the end! How wonderful does it feel to be able to run for 10 minutes without stopping? Well Done and Good Luck with your running!

The next section takes you from 10 to 55 minutes and from 5K to 10K. Don't forget to Warm up and Cool down

Training Session 1 - 40mins
Run 9 minutes, Walk 1 minutes.   Do this 4 times.

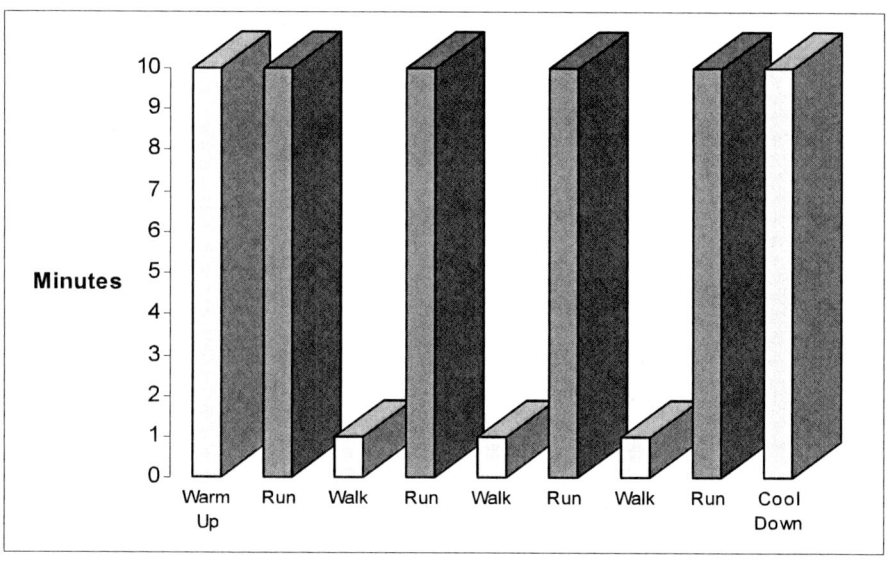

Training Session 2 - 44mins
Run 10 minutes, Walk 1 minutes.   Do this 4 times.

Training Session 3 - 44mins
Run 10 minutes, Walk 1 minutes.   Do this 4 times.

TEACH ME: How to Run

CHAPTER 2: Training Guide

How to increase your running to 10K

By now you will easily be able to run/walk 5K or 10K.
If you would like to increase your stamina so you can run the whole 10K - Here is your guide. You may have a particular race in mind, if this is the case, try and give yourself 12 weeks.
Don't forget to work in Recovery or you will be too exhausted and find it gradually harder and harder to complete the training.
Good Luck.

WEEK 1
Training Session 1 - 36mins
Run 11 minutes, Walk 1 minute.   Do this 3 times.

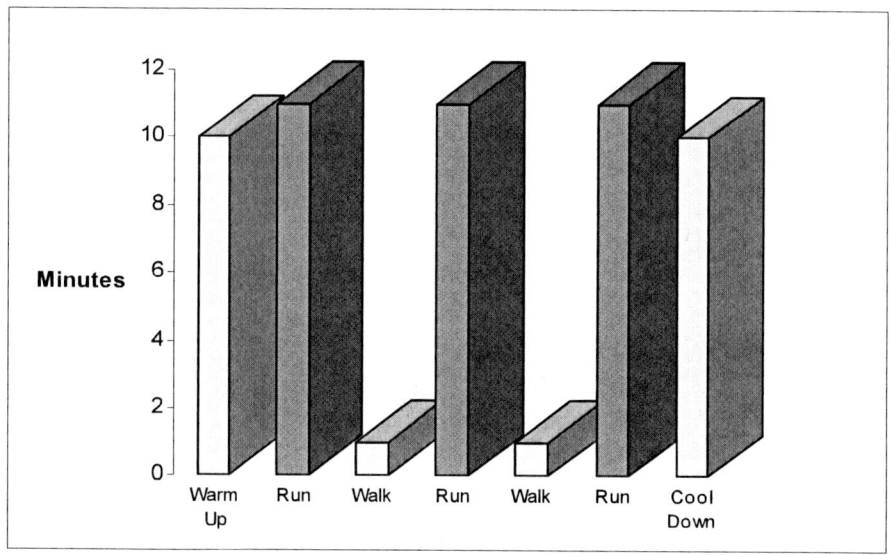

Training Session 2 - 36mins
Run 11 minutes, Walk 1 minute.   Do this 3 times.

Training Session 3 - 36mins
Run 11 minutes, Walk 1 minute.   Do this 3 times.

TEACH ME: How to Run

WEEK 2

Your body is starting to adapt to the increased mileage. Map out a 10K route and each week you will find you will be able to get a little further!
As you are running this week, think about your breathing, in through the nose, out of the mouth, in 2 second intervals.
Warm up and Cool down.

Training Session 1 - 39mins
Run 12 minutes, Walk 1 minutes.   Do this 3 times.

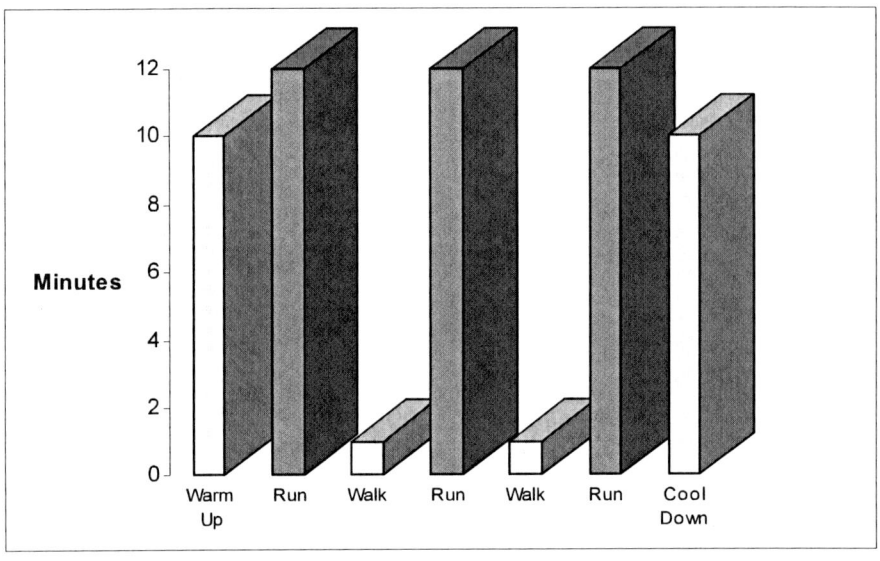

Training Session 2 - 39mins
Run 12 minutes, Walk 1 minutes.   Do this 3 times.

Training Session 3 - 39mins
Run 12 minutes, Walk 1 minutes.   Do this 3 times.

CHAPTER 2: Training Guide

WEEK 3

This is where the training starts to change. You will be doing different training at each session. The training is now adjusting to 2 shorter runs during the week and a longer run at the weekend. The objective is to have your longest run on the day of the week where you can have the most recovery. If you want to race, this should be a Sunday. This allows the body to adapt to longer runs on that day.
Warm up and Cool down.

Training Session 1 - 28mins
Run 13 minutes, Walk 1 minutes.   Do this 2 times.

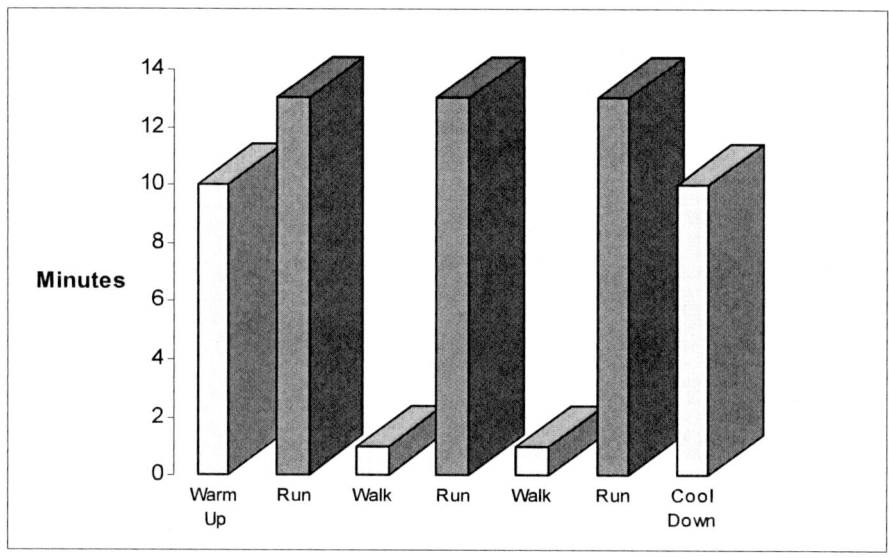

This chart shows the long run – training session 3

Training Session 2 - 26mins
Run 13 minutes, Walk 1 minutes. Run 12 minutes.

Training Session 3 - 42mins
Run 13 minutes, Walk 1 minutes.   Do this 3 times.

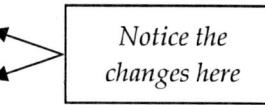

Notice the changes here

TEACH ME: How to Run

WEEK 4

This week I would like you to try and run some hills on either your training session 1 or 2. In most cases, whichever race or route you run, there will be hills of some sort. Try and lean into the hill as you run up with small steps. Stand tall as you run down and try not to lean back as this puts increased pressure on your lower back. Also avoid sprinting down as you can hurt your knees, and most importantly, lose your footing and fall!
Warm up and Cool down.

Training Session 1 - 32mins
Run 15 minutes, Walk 1 minutes.   Do this 2 times.

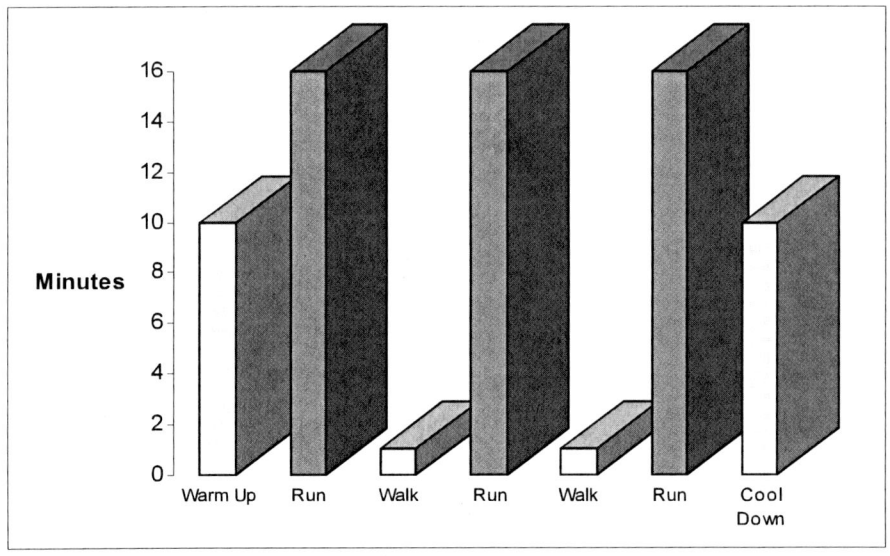

This chart shows the long run – training session 3

Training Session 2 - 29mins
Run 15 minutes, Walk 1 minutes. Run 13 minutes.

Training Session 3 - 50mins
Run 16 minutes, Walk 1 minutes.   Do this 3 times.

CHAPTER 2: Training Guide

WEEK 5
When completing your training sessions this week, I would like you to focus on your body and learn to tune in to any warning signs of a potential injury. Read Chapter 3 on Injury Prevention and particularly the section on Your Prevention Plan.
Be pro-active not re-active!
Warm up and Cool down.

Training Session 1 - 38mins
Run 18 minutes, Walk 1 minutes. Do this 2 times.

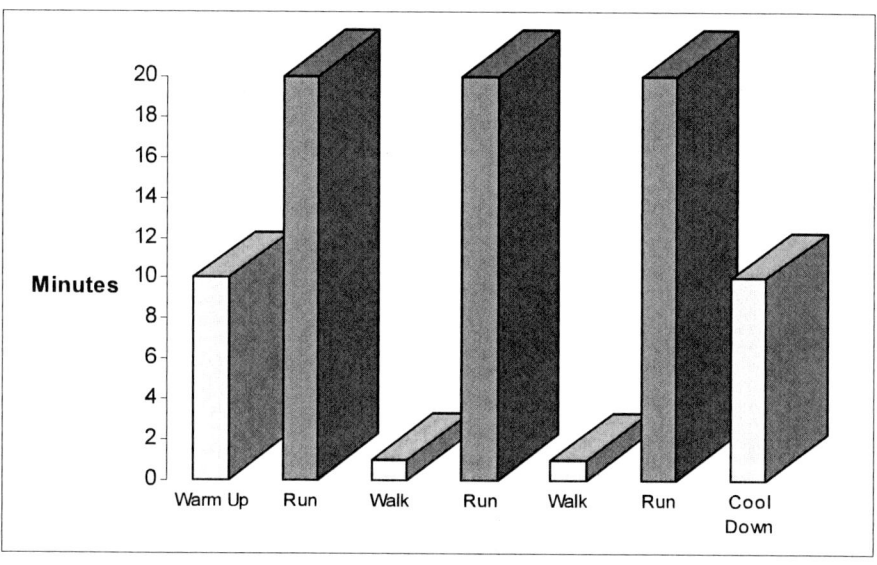

This chart shows the long run – training session 3

Training Session 2 - 31mins
Run 16 minutes, Walk 1 minutes. Run 14 minutes.

Training Session 3 - 62mins
Run 20 minutes, Walk 1 minutes. Do this 3 times.

TEACH ME: How to Run

WEEK 6

Your training changes this week so you can start to increase your long runs. Try and focus on keeping your shoulders down and your arms at your sides. Drive forward with your arms and be conscious of not allowing them to cross the body. When the arms cross the body, the Obliques are activated and you use energy on using them instead of running!
Warm up and Cool down.

Training Session 1 - 41mins
Run 20 minutes, Walk 1 minute.   Do it 2 times.

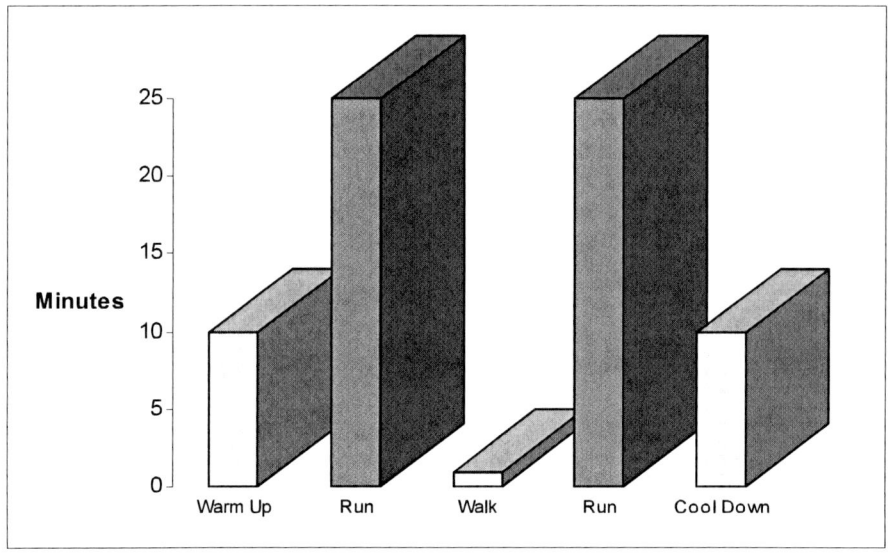

This chart shows the long run – training session 3

Training Session 2 - 31mins
Run 22 minutes, Walk 1 minute. Run 8 minutes.

Training Session 3 - 51mins
Run 25 minutes, Walk 1 minute.   Do this 2 times.

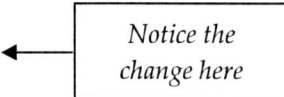

Notice the change here

CHAPTER 2: Training Guide

WEEK 7

This week is the time to focus on Stretching. We all know we need to do it but getting around to it is another matter! Make a conscious effort this week to make time for stretching. Try to do some of the stretches while watching TV in the evening or turn off the TV, put on some music, and have a 20 minute stretching session. Better still, sign up for a yoga class. Warm up and Cool down.

Training Session 1 - 41mins
Run 20 minutes, Walk 1 minute. Do this 2 times.

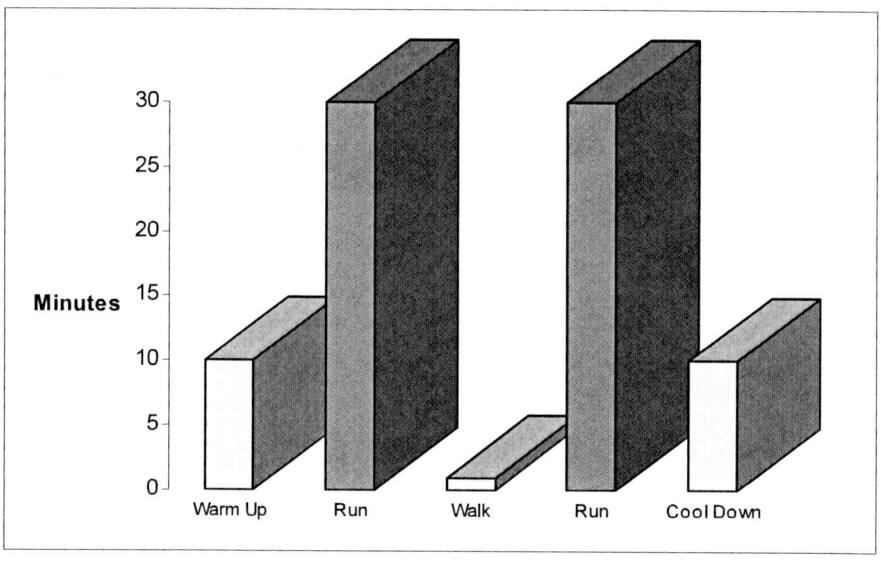

This chart shows the long run – training session 3

Training Session 2 - 30mins
Run 30 minutes.

Training Session 3 - 61mins
Run 30 minutes, Walk 1 Minutes. Do it 2 times.

TEACH ME: How to Run

WEEK 8

Your body is beginning to adapt to running for longer so your focus this week should be on Recovery. Read Chapter 6 on Rest and Recovery and see if you can implement any of the items listed. If there can only be one, then it should be your Nutrition and Hydration. Eating the right foods and drinking enough fluids, regenerates the body for your next training session.
Warm up and Cool down.

Training Session 1 - 41mins
Run 20 minutes, Walk 1 minute.   Do it 2 times.

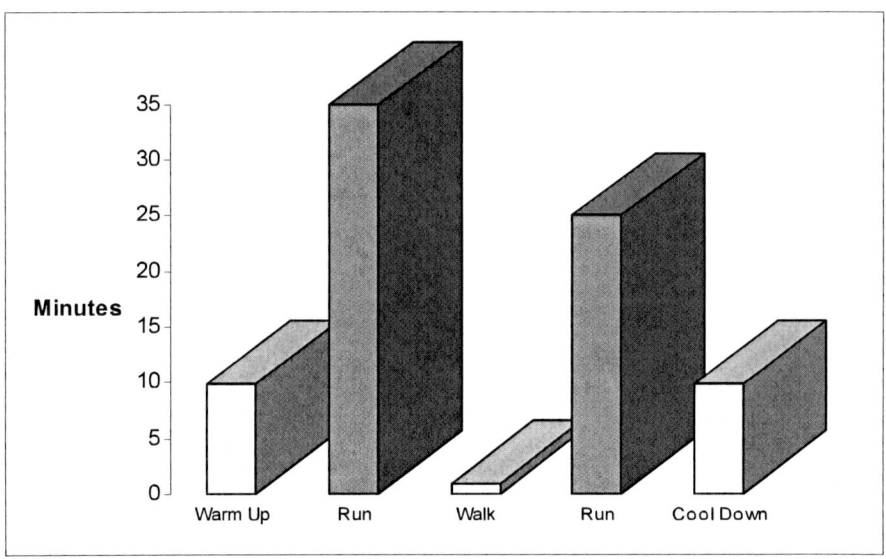

This chart shows the long run – training session 3

Training Session 2 - 30mins
Run 30 minutes.

Training Session 3 - 61mins
Run 35 minutes, Walk 1 minute, Run 25 minutes.

CHAPTER 2: Training Guide

WEEK 9

When completing your training sessions this week, I would like you to focus on your posture and core stability. Read the chapter on Core Stability and try to activate your core muscles as you run. If you activate every time you think about it whether running or not, in 6 weeks you could have a stronger core without even being aware of the effort!
Warm up and Cool down.

Training Session 1 - 41mins
Run 20 minutes, Walk 1 minute.   Do it 2 times.

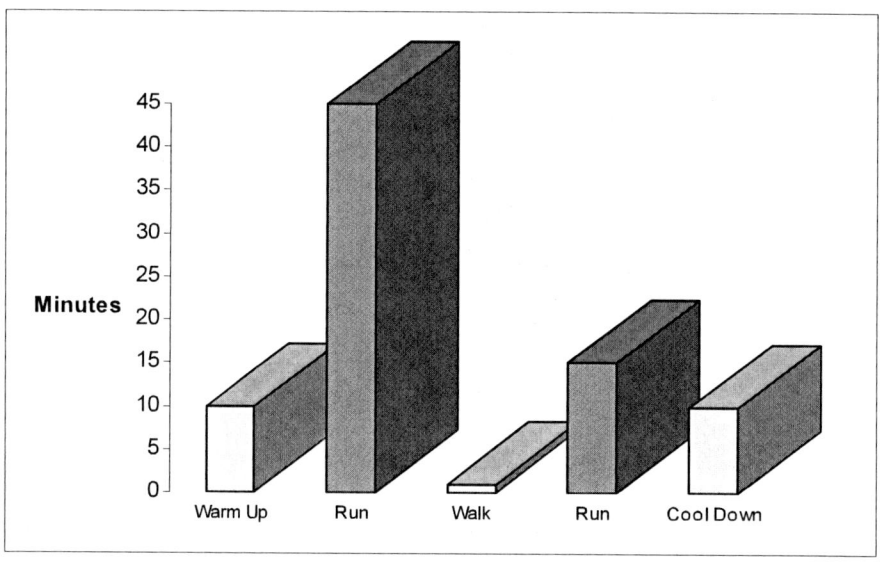

This chart shows the long run – training session 3

Training Session 2 - 41mins
Run 20 minutes, Walk 1 minute. Do it 2 times.

Training Session 3 - 61mins
Run 45 minutes, Walk 1 minute, Run 15 minutes.

TEACH ME: How to Run

WEEK 10

This is your hardest week, with the highest volume. Once you have completed this week, the volume and time diminishes as you taper for the race. You need to get through this to build up your endurance so you can complete the race. Never run more than 10K before your race – leave it for race day.

Warm up and Cool down.

Training Session 1 - 41mins
Run 20 minutes, Walk 1 minute. Do this 2 times.

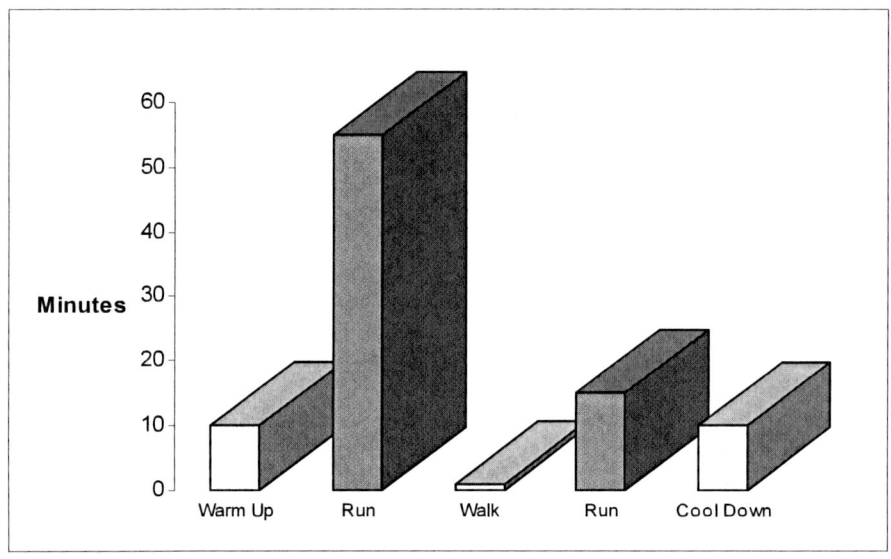

This chart shows the long run – training session 3

Training Session 2 - 30mins
Run 30 minutes.

Training Session 3 - 70mins
Run 55 minutes, Walk 1 minute, Run 15 minutes.

CHAPTER 2: Training Guide

WEEK 11

Training this week is reduced so you can perform well in the race. From now until the race, try and focus on getting enough recovery so the body can regenerate. Read the chapter on Recovery and implement what you can to aid your regeneration. Don't try any new foods or brake in new runners. The last thing you want is an unset stomach or a blister in race week!
Warm up and Cool down.

Training Session 1 - 41mins
Run 20 minutes, Walk 1 minute. Do this 2 times.

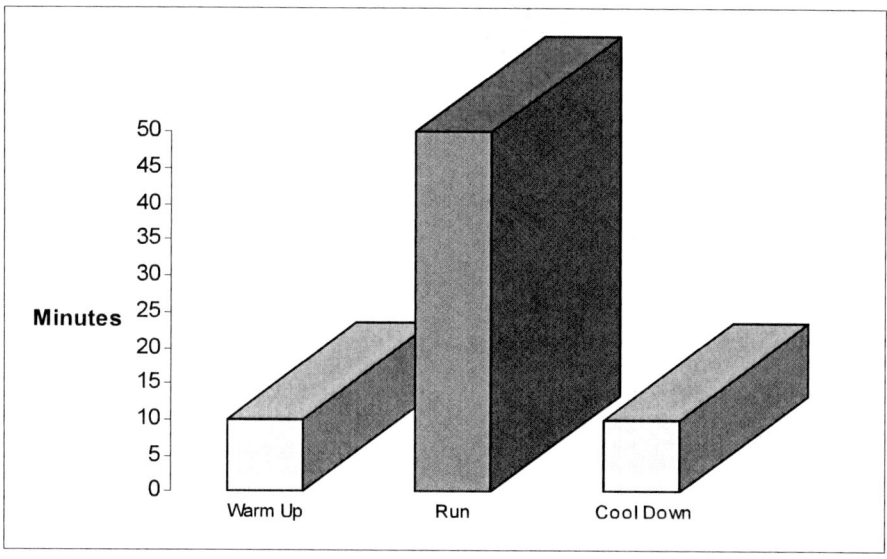

This chart shows the long run – training session 3

Training Session 2 - 30mins
Run 30 minutes.

Training Session 3 - 50mins
Run 50 minutes.

WEEK 12

This is Race week. Read Chapter 9 on Race Day Preparations as it gives you all the tips to help you plan your race.

2 days before the race - NO RUNNING. Give your body a chance to recover and regenerate so you will feel energised on race day. Check out the chapter on Nutrition which highlights details about food race day preparations. Don't forget to hydrate as well; there should be water stations on the course. Lastly, warm up before your race and treat it like any other run.

Good Luck to you.

Training Session 1 - 30mins
Run 30 minutes.

Training Session 2 - 20mins
Run 20 minutes.

2 Days before Race
Rest

1 Day before Race
Rest

Race Day
Have fun and enjoy yourself – you have worked hard enough for it!!

Chapter 3 – Injury Prevention

What is an injury?
DOMS – Delayed onset of Muscle Soreness
What do I do if I get an injury?
Running Injuries – How to avoid them.
Your Prevention Plan - Reduce the risk of an injury.

Most beginners won't experience an injury if you follow the training plan I wrote in Chapter 2. Injuries tend to happen because the runner is doing something different than they normally do. This would include things like: increasing the distance suddenly, increasing the number of runs per week, a fall, the ankle twists over, not stretching etc. I must reiterate how important consistent, slow increases and stretching are to the beginning runner. The body is suddenly experiencing new forces that put new strains on the body.

There are a number of things you can do that will prevent injuries. In this chapter I will cover what an injury is, how they occur and the most common running injuries.

What is an injury?

Injury prevention is achieved by ensuring the body is at its maximum resistance, as a result of being well maintained. Flexible muscles and joints are most important, along with the correct clothing and footwear, correct technique, training and recovery.

Flexible muscles and maximum range of motion in the joints are all essential factors in preventing injury. As you learn to run, the muscles are used differently than they have been before and they start to tighten up. This tightening never happens evenly across the whole muscle, but usually in one spot. If not released, over time, this can pull the body out of alignment, where it always finds the weakest spot of soft tissue. It locks up, seizes or tears and this is when the pain arrives! Sharp pain is an indicator that you need to stop straight away. If you carry on you could cause further damage. The key here is to Ice as quickly as possible. This reduces the swelling and starts the healing process much quicker than if you leave it until later!!

But as a beginner, it is hard to tell what is the start of a painful injury or just general muscles soreness. The rule of thumb is soreness would most likely be DOMS, whereas a sharp pain is possibly an injury.

DOMS – Delayed Onset of Muscle Soreness

As the muscle contracts it produces a substances called Lactic Acid. It is not actually an acid, per se, or it would eat the muscle away!

Lactic acid is produced as a waste product during the chemical reaction when the body converts fuel into energy. As your body produces this waste product, it can clear it away at the same speed as it is produced. That is, until you push the body for example by running or exercising. Slowly the waste starts to build up and the body can't remove it all quickly enough so the residue is left in the muscles. This is the soreness you feel after you have had a good workout or have exerted your muscles.

The trick is to clear the residue after your workout without having to exercise again. This is achieved by flushing the muscle during your cool down. This soreness is not an injury but a mere result of using your muscles.

What to do if I do get an injury?

Does this mean I have to give up running?

Most sport injuries that occur while running affect the soft and connective tissues of the body, in particular, the musculoskeletal system. Ligaments, tendons and joints are the most vulnerable to strains or sport injuries especially in the ankles and knees. Swelling and slight tenderness can result following minor tears, partial ruptures, full ruptures and sprains. Symptoms include obvious swelling, bruising and often difficulty or an inability to walk properly.

An "Avulsion" is the term given to a severe sprain when the ligament comes away from the bone. Internal bleeding, joint instability and extreme swelling along with muscle soreness, spasms and pain are the result of such injuries. If you do experience an injury, traditional treatments are best by simply resting the affected area, using cold compress, ice packs or wrapping the damaged area with a compression bandage. An excellent way to promote healing is by keeping the affected body part raised and immobilised. Resting at this time is very important to ensure that any damage to the body is repaired. Pretending the pain isn't there and carrying on as before, only prolongs the healing process. If the pain doesn't subside within a day or two it is best to see a Physiotherapist, Chiropractor or Massage Therapist or finally a Physician after prolonged pain.

Immediate treatment of an injury can reduce the severity, promote faster healing and ensure no further complications occur.

Running Injuries - how to avoid them

There are three common injuries that runners experience. All three of these are a combination of muscle tightness and over extending yourself.

Prevention is so much better than cure!!

1. **Ilio-tibial (IT) band friction Syndrome**
2. **Shin Splints**
3. **Plantar Fasciitis**

CHAPTER 3: Injury Prevention

1. Ilio-tibial (IT) band friction Syndrome

The iliotibial band is a thick band of tissue that extends from the thigh, down over the knee and attaches to the tibia. When the knee bends and straightens the iliotibial band slides over the bony part (femoral epicondyle) of the outer knee. At the bony point there is a sac of fluid called a bursa that protects the band from wearing on the bone. Unfortunately this muscle/tendon is very poorly designed for running as with each step this band rubs back and forth. Over time, if the muscle tightens up, it can put excess pressure on the bursa, which can lose its fluid and then rub on the bone. The term iliotibial band friction syndrome refers specifically to outside knee pain, irritation and inflammation of the band where it crosses the femoral epicondyle. Not everyone gets this injury. Those runners, who do, generally experience it from increased mileage, hill repeats, having bowed legs, running on a track (as you are only running one way), muscle imbalances or weak hip muscles.

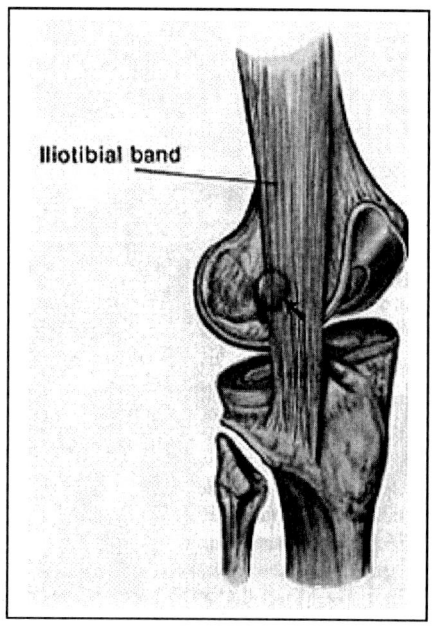

Treatment and Prevention: Rest, ice, stretch and strengthening the opposing muscles. Also check that your shoes are not worn out, and that they are the correct kind for you. If the pain gets severe, treatment from a Physiotherapist or Sports Chiropractor is a must. If left untreated this injury can and will terminate running for you!!!

The stretches recommended for prevention of this condition would be: Calf, Hamstring, Quadriceps, Gluts and Hips.

2. Shin Splints

Shin Splints is a general term for pain in the lower leg which can be felt in the front, on the sides, or even behind the lower leg bones. Pain in the shins can be for a number of reasons but true shin splints are when the muscles that insert to the tibia start to separate from the bone and/or the tibia has stress fractures, and is only experienced after many years of running. The most common shin pain is from what is known as medial tibial stress syndrome.

There are three main causes of shin pain:
1. Strain of the tibailis posterior muscle (most common).
2. Strain to the tibialis anterior muscle.
3. Stress fractures of the tibia (main weight bearing bone of the lower leg).

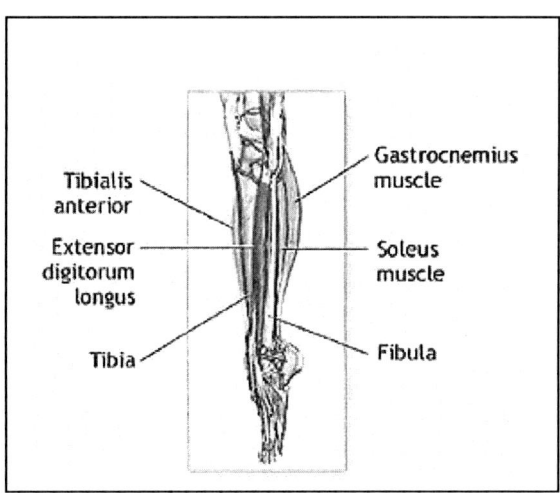

1. Strain of the tibailis posterior muscle.
The tibialis posterior muscle assists in holding up the arch of the foot; wearing footwear without enough arch support will allow the arch to drop too far and too fast and is called over pronation. As the arch drops, it pulls on the tendon that attaches the tibialis posterior muscle to the bone, placing

increased strain on the muscle. This pain can be felt just to the inside and behind of the ridge made up by your tibia on the front of your leg.

2. Strain to the tibialis anterior muscle.
The tibialis anterior muscle pulls your foot and toes upwards and is called dorsi-flexion. As the heel strikes with forces that can be up to 7 times your body weight, the forefoot and toes want to slap down hard. This tendency is reduced by a quick contraction of the tibialis anterior pulling up on the forefoot and toes causing the condition. Tight calf muscles also add to the situation. Tibialis anterior pain can be felt to the front and outside of the same tibial ridge.

3. Stress fractures of the tibia.
Stress fractures of the tibia occur after "training through the pain" and are the true shin splints. Stress fractures are fractures or breaks that do not pass completely through the bone. This pain will be felt by touching directly on the tibial ridge in front of the lower leg. These may or may not show up on x-rays, and will show up on a special imaging test called a bone scan.
If the strain to the tibialis anterior or posterior muscle is severe enough, pain directly on the tibia itself will be present, even in the absence of stress fractures, but could be as a result of the muscle separating.

Treatment and Prevention: Icing and stretching. Shin splints could be from improper or incorrectly fitting shoes, over-striding during running, over pronation of the feet (feet turning out) or lastly tight calf muscles. Going for an assessment and treatment is vital. Strengthening the muscles of the feet will help with exercises such as heel walking, toe circles, toe raises and foot circles.

3. Plantar Fasciitis

is an inflammation of the plantar fascia. "Plantar" means the bottom of the foot; "Fascia" is a type of connective tissue, and "itis" means "inflammation". Heel spurs are soft, bendable deposits of calcium that are the result of tension and inflammation in the plantar fascia attachment to the heel. Heel spurs do not cause the pain. The pain is caused by the tightness of the muscle pulling on the fascia.

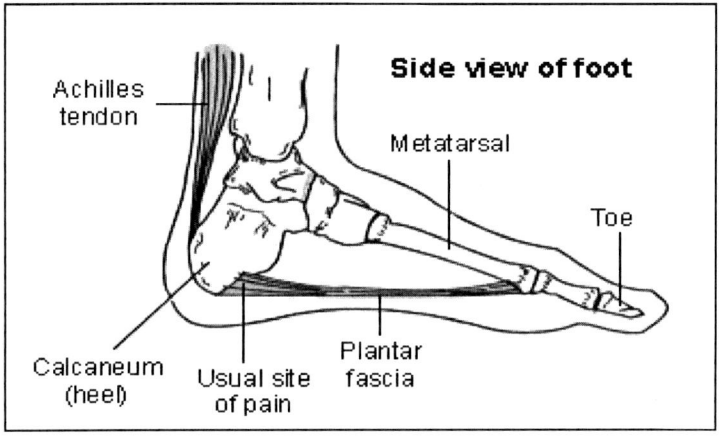

The pain is described as sharp pain in the bottom of your foot, worse in the morning upon getting out of bed. Left untreated the symptoms will increase to the point of any weight bearing activity is painful.

Treatment and Prevention: Rest, Ice and treatment of the muscles. Stretching is key, as well as deep tissue massage. Plantar fasciitis is a result of tightening of the calf muscles. Check for improper or incorrectly fitting shoes. Don't delay in getting this injury treated as the longer it lingers, the longer it takes to heal!
Stretching and strengthening the Achilles is also shown to be beneficial.

Your Prevention Plan - reduce your risk of an injury

I cannot stress to you enough - that to prevent the injury is so much better than curing it. The pain and stress you will go through is not worth thinking "It won't happen to me!"
It can and will, so be pro-active not re-active!!

Here is your check list:

Shoes – make sure you have correctly fitting shoes that have firm arches, lateral support and adequate heel cushion.

Warm-Up – Mobilizing the joints and warming up the muscles are key to preventing over stretching or tearing. Walk for ten minutes to increase your heart rate slightly. This helps increase blood flow to the muscles and warms them up.

Cool-Down - After running, cool down by walking for ten minutes. This flushes the muscles and starts the removal of waste by-products.

Stretching – This should be done, separate to your training session. See stretching chapter. If the chances are you won't get to it then gentle stretches at the end of your cool down are preferable than no stretching at all!!

Strengthening exercises – these are best started after you have become a confident runner – only you will know when that is!!

Progress – Increase running distance or time, slowly and consistently.

TEACH ME: How to Run

Chapter 4 – Stretching and Flexibility

Musculoskeletal System
Composition of Muscle
How the muscle contracts
The Benefits of Stretching
Stretching Fundamentals
When to Stretch
How often should I stretch?

We all know we need to stretch, but why?   Is it really necessary?

These are the questions I get asked all the time.
Yes, we do need to stretch, and yes it is necessary!
Firstly, as we get older we lose flexibility and the ability to keep the joints mobile and the muscles malleable. According to M. Alter, the main reason is, "as a result of certain changes that take place in our connective tissues". As we age, our bodies gradually dehydrate to some extent. It is believed that "stretching stimulates the production or retention of lubricants between the connective tissue fibres, thus preventing the formation of adhesions". Secondly, as you exercise, damage occurs to the fibres called 'Hypertrophy'. When microtrauma occurs the body responds by overcompensating, replacing the damaged tissue and adding more, so that the risk of repeat damage is reduced. The body adapts and becomes more resistant to stress. Because microtrauma is physical damage to the muscle, stretching is extremely important to maintain/improve flexibility and your range of motion.

In this chapter, I will talk about what muscles are, what they are made of and how to stretch them.

Musculoskeletal System

The bones and muscles together are called the musculoskeletal system of the body. The bones provide posture and structural support for the body and the muscles provide the ability to move. In order to function, the bones are joined together by muscles, and at the point where bones connect to one another is the joint. All muscles have an origin and insertion point into the bone and this is the part of the muscle that is inflexible, described as like ribbon and called the tendon. The origin is where the tendon grows into the part of the bone called the periosteum, the outer covering of the bone, and the insertion is where the tendon is attached to the bone we want to move. The part of the muscle that connects the bones together and always goes across a joint is called the ligament. Bones, ligaments and tendons do not have the ability to make your body move, only muscles.

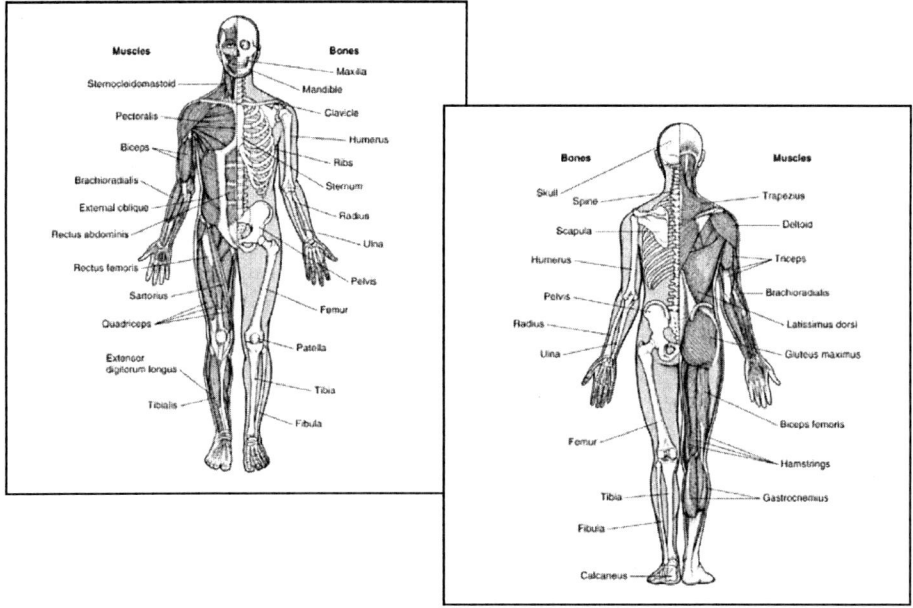

Composition of muscles

Muscles come in all shapes and sizes and provide many different purposes; however they all share the same basic structure.

There are 3 types of muscle:

Skeletal muscle: attaches to the bone and are the muscles such as quadriceps or hamstrings - they control our motion.

Smooth or involuntary muscle: we can't consciously control our smooth muscles; rather, they're controlled by the nervous system and include muscles like the stomach and intestines.

Cardiac muscle: the walls of the heart chambers.

Muscle is composed of many strands of tissue called fascicles. Each fascicle is composed of fasciculi which are bundles of muscle fibres. The muscle fibres are in turn composed of tens of thousands of thread-like myofybrils, which can contract, relax, and lengthen. The myofibrils are composed of up to millions of bands laid end-to-end called sarcomeres. Each sarcomere is made of overlapping thick and thin filaments called myofilaments. These myofilaments are made of contractile proteins, primarily actin and myosin.

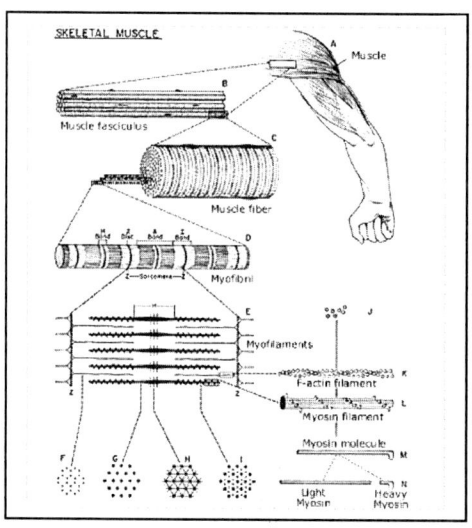

How the muscle contracts

The nerves connect the spinal column to the muscle at the neuromuscular junction. When an electrical signal crosses the neuromuscular junction it stimulates the flow of calcium which causes the thick and thin myofilaments to slide across one another. When this occurs, it causes the sarcomere to shorten, resulting in a contraction of the entire muscle fibre. When a muscle fibre contracts, it contracts completely. The more muscle fibres that are recruited by the central nervous system at a time, the stronger the force generated by the muscular contraction. Muscles cannot relax, they can only be pulled back to their original state by the opposite muscle contraction. This is why stretching is so important.

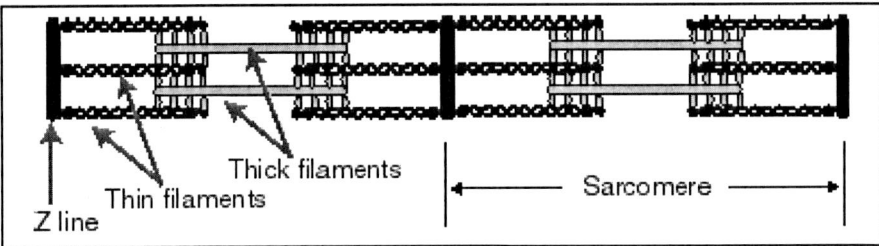

What happens when you stretch?

The stretching of a muscle starts with the sarcomere. As it stretches, this area of overlap decreases, allowing the muscle fibre to elongate. Once the muscle fibre is at its maximum resting length, additional stretching places force on the surrounding connective tissue. As the tension increases, the collagen fibres in the connective tissue align themselves along the same line of force as the tension. Hence when you stretch, the muscle fibre is pulled out to its full length sarcomere by sarcomere, and then the connective tissue takes up the remaining slack. When this occurs, it helps to realign any disorganized fibres in the direction of the tension. This realignment is what helps to rehabilitate scarred tissue back to health. The more fibres that are stretched, the greater the length developed by the stretched muscle.

Benefits of stretching

- Increased flexibility
- Improved range of motion in your joints
- Improved circulation
- Better posture
- Stress relief
- Enhanced coordination
- Reduces the likelihood of muscular soreness/fatigue
- Increases muscles efficiency/effectiveness of movement

Increased flexibility
Flexible muscles can assist your movements and action and reduce the chance of a strain or sprain.

Improved range of motion in your joints
Full range of motion is essential for coordination and balance. Maintaining the full range of motion through your joints keeps you mobile and less prone to falls, especially as you age.

Improved circulation
Stretching increases blood flow to your muscles providing the nourishment and disposal of waste by-products needed by the tissues. Improved circulation helps shorten your recovery time when you have an injury.

Better posture
Frequent stretching helps maintain good posture. Tight muscles can pull the body out of alignment and put an excessive load on the tissue increasing your risk of injury.

Stress relief
Stretching relaxes tight, tense muscles that often occur as a result of stress.

Enhanced balance and coordination
Stretching maintains balance and coordination by releasing built up tension that could lead to an imbalance and result in a fall or injury.

Reduces DOMS
Although not proven, it is believed to reduce the soreness associated with DOMS – delayed onset of muscles soreness.

Increases muscles efficiency/effectiveness of movement
Stretching can improve your overall speed, stamina, and form by enhancing the ability of muscles to contract more powerfully and economically. It can also help to lengthen your stride.

CHAPTER 4: Stretching and Flexibility

Stretching fundamentals

How to stretch?

Stretches to improve your flexibility focus on the major muscle groups: calf, thigh, hip, lower back, neck and shoulder. Here are some tips on how to make the best of your stretching.

Warm the muscles
Stretching muscles when they're cold increases the risk of a pulled muscles. Mobilise the joints first with gentle movements which lubricate the joints with synovial fluid and protects the surface of your bones - rotate the wrists and ankles, bend the arms and legs, roll your shoulders and rotate at your waist. This also increases blood flow around the body.

Hold each stretch
It takes time to lengthen tissues safely. Hold the stretch until you feel the muscle loosen off, then hold for a further 15 seconds. This should be around 30 seconds — and longer for a really tight muscle or problem area. For most muscle groups, if you hold the stretches for 30 seconds, you will only need to do each stretch once.

Don't bounce
Bouncing as you stretch causes all sort of damage. As you bounce the muscle is stretched further than its normal range which can damage the connective tissue or insertion points. It also disables the stretch reflex which is the muscles reflex action to prevent being damaged.

Stretching should be pain free
If you feel pain as you stretch, you've gone too far. You will feel a slight discomfort as the muscle is elongated but not pain. Reduce the pull to the point where you don't feel any pain, and hold it there.

Relax and breathe
Try not to hold your breath while you're stretching. Relax, and try to release the tension you can feel in the muscle.

Stretch evenly
Make sure your range of motion for the joints, is equal on both side of your body.

When to stretch

Research shows that stretching before your activity doesn't prevent injury and can, in fact, cause injury due to the inflexibility of cold muscles. Given the choice, it is preferable to stretch two hours after any activity. If there is no chance of that happening then the preference is to stretch after the exercise or run. The theory is that as you exercise the muscle, it receives damage in the form of a mircotears. If you then pull the muscle further while stretching, it causes the microtears to get bigger. The bigger the tear the longer it takes the body to repair. Waiting a few hours and allowing the muscles to start recovery and repairing the mircotears means they will repair quicker and you will gain much more from your stretching.

How often should I stretch?

Ideally three times a week. Realistically as often as you can!
Stretching is something you can easily do anytime, anywhere. At home, in your office, or even when you're travelling. Stretching for an hour once a week is the same as 3 times for 20 minutes.
If you exercise routinely but have a problem area, such as tightness in the hamstring, it would be fine to stretch every day or even twice a day. Stretching is not advised if you have certain types of injuries such as a strained muscle. If you have an injury or have a chronic condition, talk with your doctor or a physical therapist who will advise you.

CHAPTER 4: Stretching and Flexibility

Stretch Exercises for the runner

I have detailed below the stretches I would recommend for the runner. You need to concentrate on the legs but remember you also use the core and arms.

Shoulder Raises
Raise shoulders to the ears, then lower.

Arms Wide
Bicep Stretch – arms out to the sides, palms forward, move your arms back.

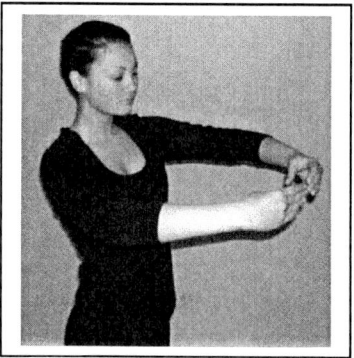

Hug a Tree
Deltoids and trapezius stretch – keep elbows out and push away from the body.

Triceps
Hand between your shoulder blades and other hand on the elbow. Gently ease the elbow backwards. Keep the chin up.

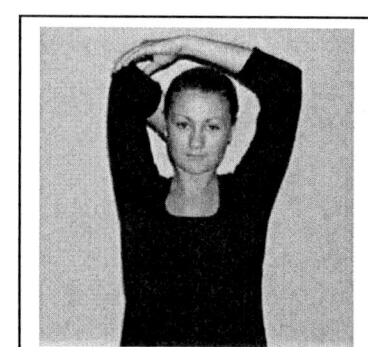

TEACH ME: How to Run

Obliques
Run your hand down the side of your thigh as you reach over your head.

Gluts
Cross leg over thigh and put arms around the other thigh and gently pull your thigh towards you.

Hip Flexors
Lunge down but keep a straight back and hips forward.

CHAPTER 4: Stretching and Flexibility

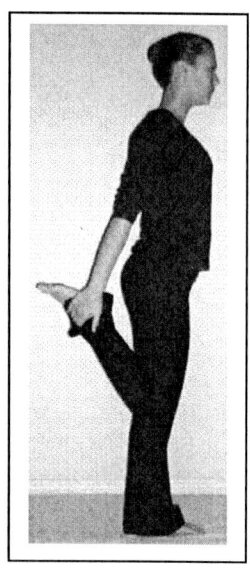

Quadriceps
Hold your ankle and gently pull your foot towards your butt. Hips forward and knees together.

Hamstrings
Bend down and rest on your heel. Keep your knee bent and stretch the back of your thigh. Push foot to the floor after about 15 seconds.

Calves
Rest your toes against a wall and push knee into the wall.

TEACH ME: How to Run

Chapter 5 – Nutrition and Hydration

Nutrition
How to Boost your Energy
Hydration
Sport Drinks
Protein Shakes
Race Day Preparations

Food – it is so much more than the fuel we need to operate the body!! It supports your heart and lungs, nourishes your cells, keeps your bones strong, hair, nails and skin healthy while also giving us the energy to run! I talk about Nutrition and Hydration in this chapter, to inform you of its importance to your recovery. I also cover Sports Drinks, Protein Bars and Shakes and how good they are - if at all!!

Traditional Food Pyramid

Vegetarian Food Pyramid

Nutrition

Carbohydrates, Proteins and Fats make up the three major building blocks known as micronutrients.

Carbohydrates

Everybody knows carbohydrates as "carbs" and believes them to be pasta, rices and the grains. Carbs also include fruits and vegetables and some of the milk groups because of the milk sugars or lactose they contain. Carbohydrate means carbon and water, hence the name. They are sugar based products and can be either simple or complex carbohydrates, depending on the amount of molecules in their chain. A simple carb can be broken down very quickly into energy whereas a complex carb takes longer.

Carbs are considered the main source of energy for the body and when they are broken down, they produce glucose, which is converted into energy and used by the body to function.

It is considered between 50-55% of your food intake should be carbs. The best sources of carbs are fruits and vegetable because of the vitamins and minerals that they also provide. Beware, excess carbs are converted to fat and stored for later! Too many carbs in the form of grains such as bagels, sandwiches, muffins, scones, energy bars or granola tend to be high in fat and sugar content and unfortunately low on quality!!

Proteins

Proteins are the building blocks of the body. They are needed for muscle growth and maintenance, supporting the immune system, maintaining strong bones, making neurotransmitters that send all the signals throughout the body and also produce enzymes that help digest food. Proteins from animals contain all building blocks of the essential amino acids your body needs, whereas vegetable proteins don't have them all. It is vital therefore to have a combination of the both. But what about vegetarians how do they get their animal amino acids? Eating eggs and fish, and drinking milk, provides them with the required animal amino acids.

Protein should form about 20% of your diet and is found in meats, milk, beans, cheese, nuts, and grains such as rice and macaroni. Breads also have protein but in a lesser amount.

Too much protein is converted to fat and can cause problems with your joints and kidneys, whereas too little protein can strip the body of nutrients! How do you get the balance right? Ideally, 1 gram of protein per kilogram of body weight. A simple way to measure this is to include 3-4 ounces of protein food at each meal a day, which is enough to fill the palm of the hand.

Fats

Fats are essential for optimal health and are a key element in the cells of our nerves, brain and spinal cord. It also plays a role in temperature control, helps protect the internal organs including the kidneys and liver and is involved in the production of our fat soluble vitamins. The goal is to keep fat intake to under 30% of your diet. The average adult male needs approximately 90 grams, whereas females 65 grams. Most diet programmers recommend a much lower fat content. While this initially results in weight loss, it can't be sustained by the body for long periods so it starts to store the fat instead and the weight loss slows down!

Fats come in two forms saturated and unsaturated. Saturated fats, which are solid at room temperature, tend to be animal fats but can also be hydrogenated fat. Hydrogenated fats from its manufacturing process are not solid at room temperature and are the "Trans Fats". The reason food manufactures use this fat is because it enhances the shelf life of food. Unfortunately, it increases the risk of numerous health problems two of which are heart disease and high cholesterol.

The good fats or unsaturated fats are the oils and should be used instead of saturated fats whenever possible. These include fish, olive, canola, nuts and seed oils. These oils provide the essential fatty acids needed and are vital for optimal health.

TEACH ME: How to Run

How to boost your energy

Eating for energy is the goal as it helps with all areas of your health including rest and regeneration. How do you start and what can you do?

The best place to start is to stabilize your body so throughout the day your energy level is constant and you don't feel fatigued, run down or tired. Eating small amounts of food regularly is the key to achieving this and ideally that would be by consuming a small meal every 2-3 hours. Two things happen when you leave large gaps between meals or have sporadic eating patterns. Firstly, the body thinks it is going to be starved and so it resorts to a mode where it begins conserving the fat and utilises the muscles as the main source of energy. Secondly, you experience spikes in your blood sugar levels which is when you get that feeling of a rush of energy that only lasts a short while and then you start to feel tired. The best way to avoid these spikes and maintain a stable energy level and a higher metabolic rate is by maintaining a healthy, well balanced diet consisting of small meals of complex carbs.

Your metabolic rate is the rate of energy usage, and goes up and down as energy is expended. It is lower when we are at rest, such as during sleep, and higher when we are exercising. The lower rate is the Basal Metabolic Rate (BMR) and is used as an indicator of your fitness level.

Hydration

To drink water or not to drink water! Can't I just drink Coffee instead?

We all need to drink more water!! Yes we know that - but why?
Our body consists of water at about 50-60% of our total body weight. Dehydration can be fatal and this can occur if your hydration level drops by only 9-12%.

CHAPTER 5: Nutrition and Hydration

Many of our body functions have a connection to water in some form. Red blood cells carry oxygen to organs and muscles in the bloodstream. Blood plasma, primarily water, transports nutrients, glucose, fatty acids and amino acids. It is also used for the removal of waste products such as carbon dioxide from the muscles. Hormones used in the body to regulate metabolism and muscular activity during exercise are transported through the plasma too. Through sweating, water is used by the body to regulate temperature and prevent your core body temperature from exceeding healthy levels. If your core temperature increases by just 1°C, your athletic performance drops significantly. Blood plasma volume is a major factor which determines blood pressure and cardiovascular function.

So we need plenty of water in our body to just function, but now we add in exercise!! During exercise, it is not unusual to expect to lose fluids at a rate of around 1-2% per hour. As we sweat we loose sodium and electrolytes. For the running beginner we don't need to worry too much about electrolytes. They are more of a concern when you are running half marathons and marathons where you can be sweating for long periods of time. By replacing lost fluids during exercise, it is possible to increase stamina, endurance and cardiovascular function. Lactic acid is removed more effectively and efficiently and the regulation of temperature and endurance levels will tend to be much more sustainable. It is best to drink little and often.

Drinking more than we might think we need, helps to maintain good hydration levels as we tend to feel less thirsty than our hydration levels may suggest. Urine is a good indicator of these levels as clear urine depicts good hydration levels where as dark urine suggests dehydration.

How much water do I need to drink?

I recommend that you drink 2 litres a day of just water in addition to other liquids.
The best way to achieve this goal without even trying is to drink a glass of water every time you have a meal. Add this to your routine of eating and you won't even notice it!

Sport drinks

Isotonic drinks are better for prolonged performance than just drinking water alone. They help to replace lost blood glucose and electrolytes. As I described above, I would only recommend these for long distance runners and only after working on concentration levels and after many months of trial and error!!

Sport drinks tend to be loaded with sugar (glucose) and are best used for that energy boost during a training session. If you are concerned about weight loss, stay away from them; otherwise come back to them when you are further down the road as an experienced runner. Water is best for beginners!!

Protein Shake

My best recommendation for all runners, be they beginner or experienced, is to drink HOME made protein shakes. The ready-mades are full of chemicals that you don't need and when preparing your own, you are making the flavours and tastes that you like!

The recommendation to maximise rest and recovery for the body is to consume protein within 20-30 minutes of completing your training session. This can be in the form of a protein meal or a protein shake. Again Protein Bars are full of preservatives and loaded with sugar. They are great in an emergency but protein shakes are the best!!

I would recommend making a protein shake in the morning. Drink 500ml after your training session and the rest during the day. As described above, the best way to maintain constant energy levels and blood sugar is not to get hungry. If you make up 1 litre it will last all day, curb your hunger and level out the blood sugar spikes!

To make 1 litre of Protein shake:

Start with 500ml of milk – this can be cows or soy
1 spoon of Protein powder - optional
250ml of fruit juice – any flavour
Then add fruit in any form. I always add a banana for consistency.
In addition you can add yogurt, or tofu as a replacement for milk.

Blend and put into a bottle or cup to drink.

I put this into a water bottle to carry around with me during the day. As long as you keep it cool it will last during the day. If you sip this it will help with that tired feeling that you can get in the afternoons when you could do with a nap, but it just isn't possible!!

Race day preparation

To Carbo load or not this is the question!

The recommendation you will get from other runners is to Carbo load the night before. This gives you all the energy you need for the race.
WRONG.
Apart from the fact it will slow you down with all that extra food in your stomach and probably keep you awake the night before trying hard to digest it all, this is just not true.
It you consider a normal week's food intake, you will generally be taking in what your body needs to produce the energy needed for running. If you continue eating that same diet the week of the race, and, as recommended reduce your running down to aid your recovery, you are in fact Carbo loading without even trying. Your energy intake is equal to a normal running week but your outgoing energy is dramatically reduced to taper down for the race so you are loading without the massive intake of food!
The best preparation for the race is to eat as normal but to include complex carbohydrates in your diet, that take longer to digest giving you a steady release of glucose into your body.

Chapter 6 – Rest and Recovery

What is Rest & why do I need to be Recovered?
Recovery Options
Sleep
Reducing Stress
De-Stressing Techniques

The key to recovery is to get the right amount of rest, hydration, and nutrition, relaxation, reducing your stress and sleep so you can start your next training session fully charged and ready to perform.

During your training session a certain amount of fatigue appears to be necessary to achieve the development of physical abilities. Fatigue is usually a temporary condition that disappears within a few hours. You need to tune into your body so you can understand the process of adaptation and recovery and this is the main aspect of this chapter. I also talk about sleep and how important it is, and, how to reduce your stress levels.

What is rest and why do I need to be recovered?

Rest and Recovery is not just sleeping or relaxation, but how the body regenerates itself between training sessions.

Optimizing your regeneration is the key to maximizing your training!

Recovery is one of the most important components of exercising and the most overlooked by the runner.
Everyone can feel the benefits of exercising while out on a run, cycle or swim but many don't realise that the benefits occur long after your training has finished. Only then, the body can start to repair the muscles and connective tissue broken down during training, as well as replenishing the energy stores that have been depleted. Also, if full recovery is permitted, an increase in the energy producing enzymes in the muscles is produced generating further improvement.

The main energy source used during exercise is Glycogen. Once training is completed it takes between 24 – 48 hours for the body to fully replenish glycogen back into the muscles. The first 2 hours are the most critical, as during this time your body can very rapidly restore this glycogen. To take advantage of this 2 hour window and assist faster recovery, it is recommended you consume some form of protein and carbohydrates within 30 minutes of finishing your training. After that time your body can't replace glycogen as quickly, and your recovery slows down.

Another thing to consider with reference to recovery - if you think about how much time you spend exercising during the week – say 3 hours? You realise that most of your time is spent in the rest and recovery phase. The problem is; how you use that time? Most of us have a busy lifestyle with lots to do during the day. Add to that children, a job, socializing while also trying to fit in some exercise, stretching, core stability, maybe some cross training or

CHAPTER 6: Rest and Recovery

weight training - we never have enough time to properly recover. What can we do?

Well there are many treatments available which can help. It may seem like you are adding to the load but in the long run they will help with recovery and regeneration of the body.

Most importantly is **Nutrition and Hydration.**

Nutrition –

plays a huge role in the speed and completeness of your recovery. Your body needs the raw materials to repair and restore the body's systems stressed by training, which comes from the foods we eat. Vitamins, minerals, water, protein, carbs and fats are needed in proper amounts in order to maximise recovery from training. A deficiency in even one key nutrient could slow this process right down and even grind it to a complete halt!

I cannot stress enough, how important proper nutrition is to the overall success of a fitness program and those runners, who are frustrated about their lack of progress, might find it can be traced back to this recovery factor.

Hydration –

also plays a huge role in recovery. Almost 60% of your body is made up of water and it is needed to replenish the sweat and moisture lost while exercising. In addition, if you replace the fluids during exercise, the body can remove the waste products such as carbon dioxide and lactic acid from the muscles more effectively and efficiently.

Recovery Options - Therapeutic Modalities

There are many Therapeutic options available for the fitness enthusiast to try and use. I must stress that one modality cannot be used exclusively to help with all aspects of recovery. It is necessary to be familiar with a variety of methods and their most effective application, so you can make an informed decision.

Here are some of the more common methods and applications:

Passive Rest

This refers to rest, as most of us know it. We all need between 7 and 8 hours of sleep a night and most of us would benefit from an additional short nap (30 minutes) during the day as well (some chance!). Many things can affect sleeping habits and those who do not get adequate sleep on a consistent basis will compromise their recovery. See information on "Sleep".

Active "Rest"

The word "Rest" in this context actually refers to using light activity to hasten recovery, most commonly known as the cool-down period. By doing 10-20 minutes of light aerobic activity after working out you will help to boost your recovery immediately. For example, if you jog lightly or walk briskly at no more than 60% of estimated max heart rate this helps to remove around 60% of the lactic acid built up in your muscles. Add in another 10 minutes and it will clear out an additional 25%! Now compare that to not cooling down at all; it can take up to 4 hours to completely clear the lactic acid and other metabolic wastes from the muscle tissue.

Warm-up is also considered active rest but actually refers to the activation and recovery runs taken between training sessions in a periodized program. These runs are for the more advanced athletes who are working on an annual plan. In this situation, for them, light activity will speed recovery faster than complete rest alone.

CHAPTER 6: Rest and Recovery

Massage

Massage is perhaps the oldest method of speeding recovery. It has been used for thousands of years and is one of the most accessible and useful methods available. It is used to increase blood circulation, reduce muscular fatigue, stretch muscle adhesions and knots, lower excessive swelling and increase lymphatic circulation.

It can be applied by you, rubbing on the sore or aching body part between sets as well as between training sessions, or you can receive a massage by a trainee or qualified professional. Trainee massage students have to do countless hours of massage training to receive their certification and most schools will offer clinics where you can receive an hour long, full-body massage for very reasonable cost.

Ideally, a massage at least once every few weeks will speed your recovery.

Heat (Thermotherapy)

The application of heat. This has many forms from simply taking a hot shower to sophisticated methods such as ultrasound.

Heat increases the blood flow to the targeted area with the obvious benefits of removing waste products and speeding the delivery of vital recovery nutrients such as the amino acids and vitamins. Heat should not be used immediately after training or for the treatment of an acute injury or trauma. Heat should be used for muscle soreness and not for at least 2-3 hours after your training session. It can be used in combination with cold therapy – see contrast bath.

Cold (Cryotherapy)

The application of cold. Cold therapy is another of the more popular therapeutic remedies. Its main benefit is localized pain relief without the aid of drugs and is applied either as an ice pack for small areas or a cold bath for the larger areas. It is mostly known as a treatment for injuries but equally it can be used as a recovery remedy.

Appling cold to a traumatized tissue will reduce swelling and muscle spasms and increase local blood flow which is vital to reduce the recovery time. Alternatively, if you apply cold immediately after training and every 20 minutes for no more than 2 hours this has been shown to aid recovery in tissues that requires longer regeneration periods such as fast-twitch muscles.

Contrast Bath

This is the use of heat and cold in combination and is best used to ease muscle pain (DOMS – delayed onset of Muscle Soreness) or before an injury becomes severe. The most common theory on why contrast baths work so well is that the changes between vasodilatation (heat) and vasoconstriction (cold) cause a "pumping" action in the muscles and helps speed waste removal and nutrient delivery.

Many options and recommendations exist. They include: starting or ending with cold, spending 3-4 times longer on heat treatment compared to cold treatment and what is the optimal length of time. One combination is not necessarily better than another but whichever you use they are extremely effective.

Acupuncture/Acupressure (Reflexotherapy) –

This treatment is based on the ancient Chinese concept that energy (chi) flows along channels called meridians through the body. A disruption of these meridians can interfere with the body's functions, including those that effect recovery. Reflexotherapy is used to restore
the flow and promotes healing and harmony within the body. This is achieved by adding pressure to key points along the medians. *Acupuncture* is the use of needles whereas *Acupressure* is the use of direct pressure from the fingers. It has taken many years for western doctors to accept these methods, but as research and evidence grows it is becoming more and more common and accepted.

Sleep

There is nothing more frustrating than not being able to sleep. Your mind is racing, going over everything that happened today. Night noises keep you awake. You are tossing and turning. What can you do? There ARE things you can do!

Sleep only when sleepy
This reduces the time you are awake in bed. If you can't fall asleep within 20 minutes, get up and do something boring until you feel sleepy. Sit quietly in the dark or read the warranty on your refrigerator! Try not to expose yourself to bright light while you are up as the light gives cues to your brain that it is time to wake up.

Don't take naps
This will make sure you are tired at bedtime. If you just can't make it through the day without napping, try sleeping for less than an hour and before 3 pm.

Get up and go to bed the same time every day
Even on weekends! When your sleep cycle is in a regular rhythm, you will feel much better.

Refrain from exercise at least 4 hours before bedtime
Regular exercise is recommended to help you sleep well, but the timing of the workout is important. Exercising in the morning or early afternoon will not interfere with your sleep.

Develop sleep rituals
It is important to give your body cues that it is time to slow down and sleep. Listen to relaxing music, read for 15 minutes, have a cup of caffeine free tea, do relaxation or stretching exercises.

4-6 hours before bed stay away from caffeine, nicotine & alcohol
Caffeine and nicotine are stimulants that interfere with your ability to fall asleep. Coffee, tea, cola, cocoa, chocolate and some prescription and non-

prescription drugs contain caffeine. Cigarettes and some drugs contain nicotine. Alcohol may seem to help you sleep in the beginning as it slows brain activity, but it will end up giving you fragmented sleep.

Have a light snack before bed
If your stomach is too empty, it can interfere with your sleep. However, if you eat a heavy meal before bedtime, that won't help either. Dairy products and turkey contain tryptophan, which acts as a natural sleep inducer. Tryptophan is probably why a warm glass of milk is sometimes recommended.

Take a hot bath 90 minutes before bedtime
A hot bath will raise your body temperature, but it is the drop in body temperature that triggers your sleep cycle.

Reducing Stress

Stress is one of the most destructive things that can affect the body. Individuals who are stressed have a greater chance of becoming ill and it is associated with some chronic diseases such as arthritis, gastric ulcers, and heart attacks. We all experience stress at some point in our lives. Stress is self-defined and is anything that the individual sees as stressful. It is like pain, if you say you have pain, you have pain. If an individual perceives a situation as stressful, then it is stressful to them.

At certain times we can feel more stressed than others and this is when relaxation techniques can help a great deal to minimize physical problems. Excessive muscle tension and an increase in catabolic hormones are two of the most common physical problems that can slow down recovery.

The first thing to do is to identify what is stressing you. Make a list of all the things in your life that you deem to be stressful. They may be family issues, health problems, work related situations or day to day difficulties you have to deal with. When you have your list; identify the ones you can minimize or eliminate. Talk to other people, family or friends, in fact anyone who can help you.

Pain
If you have frequent discomfort or pain, seek assistance from a physician or pain management team. Don't think you have to suffer with pain, or nurse a painful injury - get some treatment. With current advances in this area, it is usually not necessary to live with this constant stressor.

Plan Ahead
It often takes longer than you would think to make arrangements, especially when you are pressed for time. Make a list of what needs to be done and schedule each task. Then stick to the schedule and this will help to decrease last minute stresses.

Making Time for You
If you are giving care to a loved one, looking after children, have a demanding career or one of the many other demands on your time, you need to make time for yourself. Plan time away, it can either be away from the situation or just time on your own. Try to do something you really enjoy, so that you come back refreshed.

Develop a Network of Friends
Feelings of loneliness or aloneness can be a chronic stressor. Having someone to talk to or lean on during stressful times can be a life saver. Think ahead of how to find a steady stream of friends and caring individuals who can provide support. Do not rely only on a small select set of friends. Expand your mind; join a class, a group or a political party - take the opportunity to have contact with a lot of different types and ages of people.

Spread out the Stressors
Stressful situations grouped together increase the level of stress and have a cumulative effect on your health and well being. Think of ways to spread out

the events or situations that are stressful to you. While it may not be possible to plan for all the eventualities in your life, some events or situations that are stressful may be postponed, such as holidays or family visits. Try to plan for ways to decrease the number of stressors and the impact of each stressor in your life.

De-stressing techniques

There are many techniques that can be used to relieve or reduce the amount of stress in your life. Some you will find are easier than others to master but find one or two that can benefit you.

Yoga

Yoga is a wonderful stretching/flexibility/breathing/meditation session. There are many different types of yoga classes which I have listed:

Hatha - is a very general term that can include many of the physical types of yoga. If a class is described as Hatha style, it is usually slow-paced and gentle and can provide a good introduction to the basic yoga poses.

Vinyasa - which means breath-synchronized movement, tends to be a more vigorous style based on the performance of a series of poses called Sun Salutations where the movement is matched to the breath. The class will typically start with a number of Sun Salutations which warms up the body to prepare for a more intense stretching later in the class.

Ashtanga - which means eight limbs in Sanskrit, is a fast-paced, intense style of yoga. A set series of poses is performed, always in the same order and is very physically demanding due to the constant movement from one pose to the next. Ashtanga is also what is often called Power Yoga although it might not necessarily keep strictly to the set Ashtanga series of poses.

Iyengar - this style is principally concerned with bodily alignment. In yoga, the word alignment is used to describe the precise way in which your body should be positioned in each pose in order to obtain the maximum benefits of the pose and avoid injury. Iyengar practice usually emphasizes holding poses over long periods with the use of equipment such as yoga blankets, blocks and straps in order to bring the body into alignment.

Kundalini - is focused on controlling the breath in conjunction with physical movement, with the purpose of freeing energy in the lower body and allowing it to move upwards. Kundalini uses rapid, repetitive movements rather than holding poses for a long time, and the teacher will often lead the class in call and response chanting.

Bikram/Hot Yoga - is practiced in a 95-100 degree room, which allows for a loosening of tight muscles and profuse sweating, which is thought to be cleansing. The Bikram method is a set series of 26 poses, but not all hot classes make use of this series.

Visual imagery

Visual Imagery is the concept of seeing in one's mind an image, object or action as if it was right there, when in fact it is not. It can be thoughts you can see, hear, feel, smell, or taste and an inner representation of your experience or your fantasies - a way your mind codes, stores, and expresses information. Imagery is dreams and daydreams; memories and reminiscence; plans, projections, and possibilities, and most importantly, the image of your deeper self.
It is a tool often used by athletes to plan or anticipate how a race or match is going to be played and gets them psyched and ready for the event. Whereas it is also used to calm and control your emotions by taking yourself away

from the current stress or situation and allowing your mind to visualise a place of peace and harmony to calm you.

However used, this is a very powerful tool that can be used to great effect for stress relief.

Meditation

This is an ancient technique practised by many cultures and religions to find inner peace. The image of meditation though, conjures up the picture of a bearded man sitting cross-legged in front of an entrance to a cave high on a mountain top. Climbing the mountain and reaching him is part of the arduous journey toward self-fulfilment or self-improvement. Once we find him we ask, "What is the meaning of life?" or "How do we achieve peace in ourselves and our lives?" This all-knowing man tells us the answers are "inside ourselves" and tells us to go and contemplate.

Meditating is actually much easier than you might imagine. We all have experimented with a form of meditation by consciously relaxing. It may have been during an exercise class, to manage pain or calming yourself before a test.

To start, you need to pay attention to your breathing. The effort of focusing completely on your breathing takes your mind away from the "mind clutter" that constantly invades us. As you concentrate on the breathing, clear your mind and let it lead you to a time of calm. With repeated effort the goal of clearing your mind – to think of nothing – does occur and the process of meditation takes on its own energy. The result is, and I guarantee this, peace, serenity, calmness, that eventually opens you to new insights.

Positive Self Talk

The most powerful control you have on your attitude and personality is what you say to yourself and how you respond internally is what determines your thoughts, feelings, and actions. By controlling your inner dialogue, or your "self talk," you can begin to control the way you deal with the stresses and problems in your life.

CHAPTER 6: Rest and Recovery

We are constantly faced with challenges, difficulties, and problems; they are unavoidable and one of the inevitable parts of life. How you draw upon your resources and respond to each challenge will determine whether you struggle under the strain or grow and become a stronger person. When you see things positively and you look for the good in every situation and in each person, you will become a very positive and optimistic person. Since the quality of your life is determined by how you feel moment to moment, you should make it a habit to only think and talk about what you want and keep your mind off of what you don't want.

Optimistic people always talk to themselves in a positive and constructive way. Whenever they experience adversity of any kind, they take full control of their inner dialogue and counter any negative feelings by immediately reframing the event so that it appears positive in some way.

It all comes down to the way you talk to yourself on a daily basis. When a problem or difficulty comes up you must learn to change your language from negative to positive. For example, you should learn to use the word challenge instead of problem. A problem is something you wrestle and struggle with. It represents a potential loss and difficultly. A challenge, on the other hand, is just something that you rise to and that makes you stronger. The word challenge is inherently positive. The way you interpret the event to yourself is what makes it sound and appear completely different. When you are faced with a difficulty of any kind, instead of saying, "I have a problem," you should say, "I have an interesting challenge for me."

One of the common characteristics of all high achieving men and women is that they recognize the inevitability of temporary setbacks and disappointments. They accept them as a normal and natural part of their life. They do everything possible to avoid problems, but when they come up, successful people learn from them and rise above them. They continue to move forward towards their goals.

TEACH ME: How to Run

Chapter 7 – Core Stability

Core Stability – What is it and why do we need it?
Pilates
Exercises to try at home

The body's "core" as we know it, comprises of the muscles that lie deep within the torso. They attach to the pelvis, hips and spinal column while supporting the scapula and can be described as the body's girdle.
Core stability training is essential to any sports performance as it is the foundation for all movement, especially the extremities. Training these muscles will correct postural imbalances while helping to prevent injury, improve balance and coordination and develop functional fitness - that is, fitness that is essential to both daily living and regular activities.
But why do we need to have a strong core? Imagine trying to hit a ball in a game of baseball but instead of a bat you have a length of chain - try and hit the ball. This is what the body is like without a strong core. Weak core muscles cause all sort of injuries, balance and coordination problems and often people experience back pain.
When you start core stability training the object is to learn how to identify the key muscles and then how to activate them. The main muscles that we focus on are the Transversus Abdominus and Internal Obliques.
Interestingly, as early as the 1920s Joseph Pilates talked about developing a 'girdle of strength' by learning to recruit the deep-trunk muscles. Even without a complete knowledge of anatomy and the benefits of the latest muscle activity research, he was aware of the importance of these deep muscles and their supportive effects. Having identified the key muscles and how they act, the next step is how best to train them. I have taught Pilates for many years and find it to be an excellent introduction to core stability. It teaches you how to isolate the correct muscles and the slow and controlled movements gradually improve posture and coordination, body awareness, coordination and can reduce back pain.

Pilates

Pilates is a structured set of movements coordinating activation of the key muscles with the breathing and correct alignment of the pelvis. Each movement is based on the principles of Joseph Pilates and comprise of relaxation, breathing, concentration, alignment, centring, stamina, coordination and flowing movements. All the Pilates exercises are tailored for the needs of the individual and their level of fitness and, should be taken as a series of lessons in a course as opposed to a "drop in" format.

Lessons come in two formats – Mat work classes or studio based using the Reformer Tables.

Mat work tends to be in a class format and teaches you the basics of breathing correctly, stabilising your pelvis and activating the abdominal muscles while performing exercises and movements. During each lesson, more complex routines are introduced as the experience and skill level of the class members improves.

Studio sessions use a variety of specialised resistance equipment and reformer tables. These classes are usually taught on a one to one basis and include a postural assessment. A personal program is specifically designed for you and the instructor will ensure your safety and effectiveness of the workout, while using the equipment.

The foundation of the Pilates technique offers a unique method of body control and conditioning, while stretching and strengthening the muscles you will improve your flexibility, balance and coordination. The moves function differently from other forms of exercise as they concentrate primarily on strengthening the central core by using the abdominal muscles to control the movements while focusing your mind and breathing on the exercises. This, in turn, allows the body to become stronger, firmer and gradually re-aligned without building muscle mass. Physiotherapists, Osteopaths and Chiropractors have started to promote Pilates for the health improvements that can be achieved.

There are three fundamental components that need to be taught before you can start: Neutral spine, controlled breathing and activating the abdominals.

CHAPTER 7: Core Stability

Neutral Spine

Neutral spine or neutral pelvis has the same meaning, and involves finding the natural position for the spine by aligning the pelvis. This natural position is considered to be the correct alignment of the spine and exercising with the spine and pelvis in this position will; improve the posture and balance, increase your efficiency during everyday tasks and reduce the risk of back injury or posture deterioration. To find neutral start by standing up tall, shoulders down, knees slightly bent and in line with your feet, arms on your hips and lastly, chin in not jutting forward.

I describe finding your neutral position in one of two ways. The first is to imagine your pelvis bone as a bowl filled to the brim with water. If you tilt the pelvis backwards and forwards you will tip out some of the water to the front or to the back. Try and position the pelvis centrally so the water stays in the bowl.

Alternatively, or as well, stand sideway to a full length mirror and check where you arm is in relation to your thigh. As you tilt the pelvis backwards and forwards you will see the arm move forwards or backwards. Try to align the arm in the middle of the thigh.

Controlled Breathing

The breathing is always in line with your movements and try to match the speed of the exercises with your breath going in and out. Stand tall and put your finger tips together under the bust. Imagine your lungs as balloons filling up with air, and as it fills up you can feel the back of your ribs with your lungs. Keep the shoulders down and breathe using the diaphragm, like you do when you are sleeping or resting, allowing the stomach to go in and out. As you breathe in the fingers should slightly part and come back together as you breathe out. The breathing is always controlled and aligned with the movement. As you breathe out, start the movement, as you breathe in, come back to the original position.

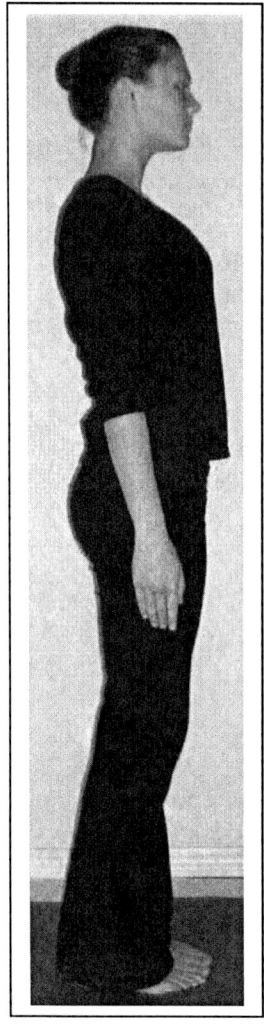

Activating the abdominals – Transverse Abdominal
Isolating these muscles is the first objective.
The Transverse Abdominals (TA) are a band of muscles along with the Internal Obliques (IO) that circle the body in a cylinder. If you then add the diaphragm as the top of the cylinder and the pelvic floor as the bottom, this is the core as we know it. We only need to activate the lower half about 6 inches from the top of the pubic bone to the top of the hip bone. I tell my students to imagine you are wearing a 6 inch belt on the hips. These are the muscles that you need to practise activating.
There are two ways to activate these muscles – you can either activate the TA's or the pelvic floor.

To activate the TA: imagine the belt around your hips and you are pulling the belt in as tight as it can go, as if it had ten holes in and you are taking it to the tenth hole. Relax off. This time only tighten to the half way – what would be say the 5th hole and ease off just a little to say the 4th hole. This is the point of activation. Learn how to tense the abdominals and relax them. If you practise this whenever you remember you could be at the point in 6 weeks where they will stay activated all the time!! They say that it only takes 6 weeks to change a habit.

To activate the Pelvic Floor (PF): imagine a lift going up inside you as you tense the pelvic floor muscles. It has 10 floors and the tenth floor is as tight as you can tense. Tense as tight as you can and then relax. Try this again but this time relax off to what would be the fifth floor and then a little less and hold there. Tense to that point and then relax. This is activating the Pelvic Floor and is equally as good as Transverse Abdominals. As I described above, the core cylinder has both the pelvic floor muscles and the transverse abdominal connected. If you activate the TA the PF will be activated and visa versa. Either way a 40% contraction is the most effective.

CHAPTER 7: Core Stability

Exercises to try at home

I have listed below 10 of the basic Pilates movements that will start you off and can be practised at home.

Swimming

Lying on the floor, lift alternative arm and leg trying not to arch the back. Breathe out on the lift, breath in as you return.

Swan Lift

Keep arms in place as you lift the chest off the floor.

Side leg lift

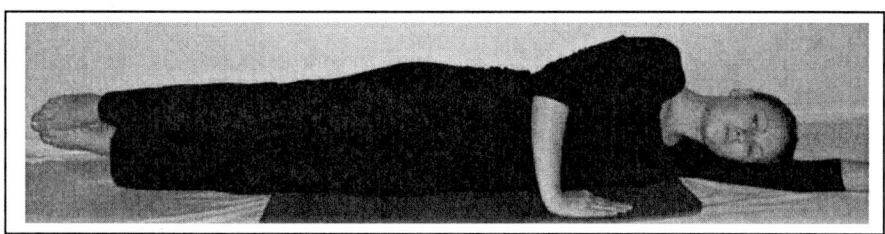

Lying on your side, keep both feet off the floor and balance. When steady practise moving the hand to rest on the thigh.

Side lift

Lying on your side resting on your arm, lift the butt off the floor.

Shoulder Bridge

Lying on your back, arms by your sides slowly raise your butt and back, one vertebra at a time, until at the top. Lower back to the floor.

CHAPTER 7: Core Stability

One leg circle

One leg straight in the air and circle slowly 3 times one way and 3 times the other, then change legs.

One leg stretch

Slowly extend leg out staying parallel to the ground and draw back to the body.

Cat Stretch –

This is a stretch to relax the muscles in between movements.

On all fours slowly arch the back and drop the head between the arms. Sink back down and raise the head.

Swimming on all fours

Push leg away from the body keeping the toes on the floor.

CHAPTER 7: Core Stability

Side Twist

Hips facing forward twist the upper body one way and then back to the centre and then the other way.

Roll Down

Slowly lower to the floor and then come back up, keeping the back rounded. Try not to go further down than you can get up from, without help.

TEACH ME: How to Run

Chapter 8 – Weight Training

Do I need to do Weight Training?
How can it help the runner?
Major Muscle Groups
The Essentials of Proper Form
Set and Reps
Progression
How often should I Weight Train
Sport Specific Exercises.

Weight Training or Strength Training is using resistance to strengthen the muscles. Weight training is also recommended to help with Osteoporosis, Arthritic Pain along with a host of other health benefits.

Ladies - it will **NOT BULK YOU UP** unless you are at the gym everyday lifting weights for 2-3 hours at a time. It will give you tone and definition and I guarantee that if you follow a training plan you will be delighted with the results. The only down side is, to see these wonderful new muscles you will need to lose the fat covering them and that is where running comes in! It doesn't happen over night! It has taken many years to add this unwanted extra weight and it will take time to remove it! Not the same amount of time as it took to put on but not 6 weeks either!

Weight training can be a little intimidating for the beginner. You might picture the gym as a sweat smelling place where huge body building types are pumping massive weights. Well it is not like that anymore and the gym has become a place where people of all ages and abilities can go and fit in.

Gyms come in all types and price brackets! From your sweaty body building gym to top of the range spa and treatment retreat! There is a gym in everyone's price range and the local recreation centre would be a good place to start.

Start with an introduction program as this gets you familiar with the equipment and how to use the machines. I am a great believer in free weights as I can use more muscles groups per exercise than the machines as they are targeted to a specific muscle. Either way it is a great way to increase your strength and prevent injury.

How can it help the runner?

Increasing your muscle mass means you will be stronger and able to run faster. The added bonus is, as your muscle mass increases it takes more calories to use these larger muscles – more fat burning.

There are an endless number of different weight training programs and theories. So where do you start and what do you do?
The foundation of a safe and effective weight training program starts with learning the major muscle groups. I have listed them below and general exercises that target that specific muscle group.
The next step is to select effective exercises for your needs; I have listed the major muscles groups and basic exercises I would recommend for the runner at the end of this chapter.
Lastly you will need to learn the essentials of proper form, what are the differences between reps and sets, how to progress and how often do I need to work out.

CHAPTER 8: Weight Training

The Major Muscle Groups

When choosing exercises for your weight training routine, it's essential to have at least one exercise for each muscle group. This avoids muscle imbalances that can lead to injury. While it is essential to cover all the major muscle groups, sport specific exercises for the runner would advise a general exercise to include all the back muscles as opposed to individually. Here are the major muscle groups, starting from the head, with the type of exercise that would be used:

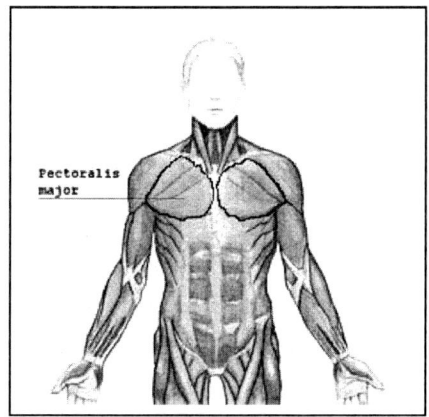

Pectoralis major
Large fan shaped muscle that covers the front of the upper chest.
Exercises: push-ups, pull-ups, regular and incline bench press, and the pec deck machine.

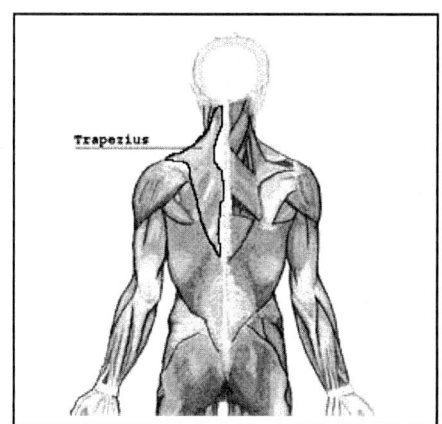

Trapezius
Upper section of the back often referred to as the 'traps.' The upper trapezius is the muscle running from the back of the neck to the shoulder.
Exercises: upright rows, and shoulder shrugs with weight.

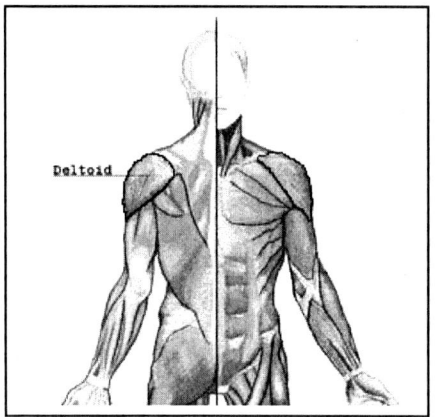

Deltoids

The cap of the shoulder. This muscle has three parts, anterior deltoid (the front), medial deltoid (the middle), and posterior deltoid (the rear). Different exercises target the different parts.
Exercises: The anterior deltoid - push-ups, bench press, and front dumbbell raises.
The medial deltoid - standing lateral dumbbell raises.
The posterior deltoid - rear dumbbell raises while seated.

Rhomboids

Muscles in the middle of the upper back between the shoulder blades.
Exercises: chin-ups, and moves that bring the shoulder blades together.

Latisimus dorsi

Mid section of the back.
Exercises: pull-ups, chin-ups, and the lat pull-down machine.

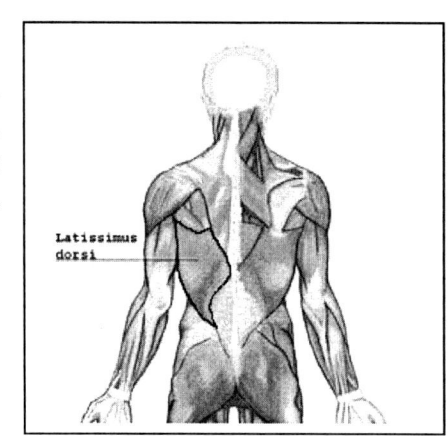

CHAPTER 8: Weight Training

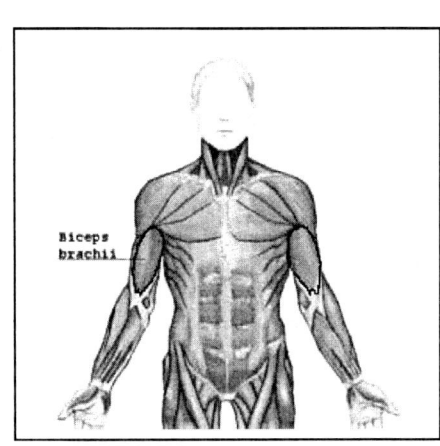

Biceps
The front of the upper arm.
Exercises: bicep curls with barbell, dumbbells, or a machine.

Lower back
There are many muscles in this section but most importantly the Erector Spinae which extends the back and aids with your posture.
Exercises: back extensions and prone back extension exercises. These muscles are also used during the squat and dead lift.

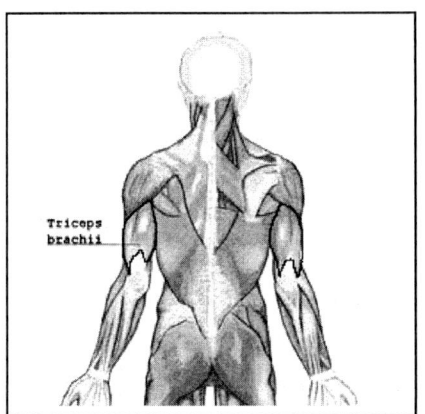

Triceps
The back of the upper arm.
Exercises: tricep dips, tricep extensions, tricep kick-backs, and overhead presses. These muscles are also used during the bench press and military press.

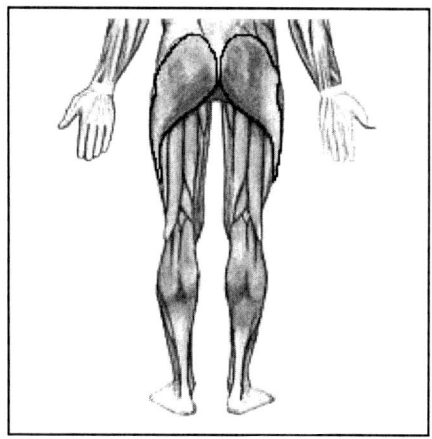

Gluteals
The group of muscles covering your butt often referred to as the 'gluts'.
Exercises: squats and leg press machine. These muscles are also used during lunges, tall box step ups, and plyometric jumps.

Abdominals
Rectus Abdominus, Transverse Abdominals, External and Internal Obliques the muscles that circle the body often referred to as the "core". Different exercises target the different parts.
Exercises: Rectus Abdominus - standard crunches and curls.
Transverse Abdominals - reverse curls and crunches where hips are lifted instead of the head & shoulders.
External & Internal Obliques: crunches involving a rotation or twist.

Hip abductors and adductors
The muscles of the inner and outer thigh. The abductors are on the outside and move the leg away from the body.
The adductors are on the inside and pull the leg across the centerline of the body.
Exercises: variety of side leg lifts while standing or lying and multi-hip machines.

CHAPTER 8: Weight Training

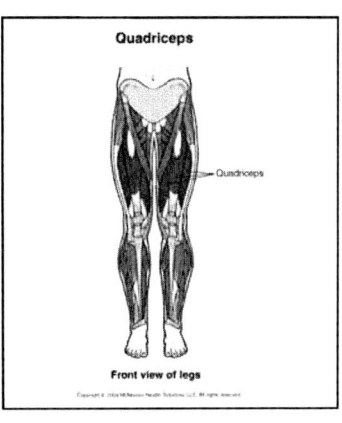

Quadriceps
This front of the thigh.
Exercises: lunges, leg extension machine, and leg press machine.

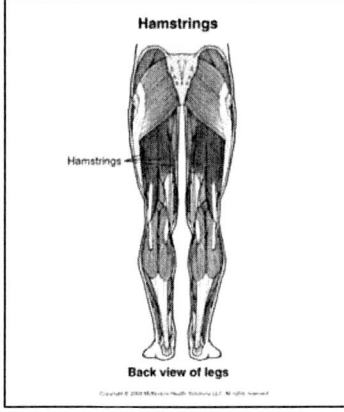

Hamstrings
The back of the thigh.
Exercises: squats, leg curl machine, lunges and leg press machine.

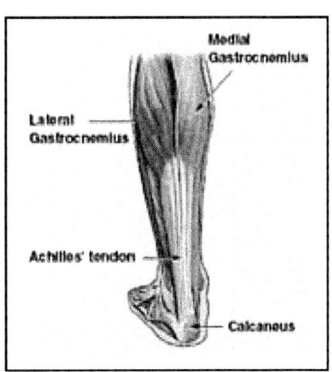

Calf
The back of the lower leg and includes the Gastrocnemius and the Soleus. The Gastrocnemius is what gives the calf its strong rounded shape and Soleus is the flat muscle running under the Gastrocnemius.
Exercise: Gastrocnemius - standing calf raises. Soleus - seated or bent knee calf raises.

97

The essentials of proper form

The correct posture when weight training is essential to prevent injury. It is strongly advised to get a professional assessment to start with and they will introduce you to the equipment. The best way to begin is by using the machines. They only allow you to do the exercise in the correct manner and to the maximum extension for the muscle. As your experience grows then would be the time to get a personal trainer and progress to the more advances techniques offered with the free weights. Correct posture includes: full range of motion, speed, form, weight, sequence and knowing when enough is enough!

Full range of motion
Full range of motion is an important component of correct form. Each exercise should be taken through the complete range of joint movement in a slow controlled manner, allowing the whole muscle to be utilized. The sarcomeres lay in straight lines in the muscle fibres and are recruited as more of the muscle is used. If you only move a small amount only a few of the sarcomere are engaged whereas if you move through the full range you recruit all the sarcomere and it benefits the whole muscle. Also when you use the full range of motion movements, as you contract and strengthen the muscle you are working (the prime mover), you also stretch the opposing (antagonist) muscle. This contributes to both muscle strength and joint flexibility.

Speed of the movement
Slow controlled movements are the most beneficial. Fast, jerky movements place undue stress on the muscle and connective tissue
at the beginning of the movement and significantly increase the likelihood of an injury. You will also find that if you are lifting at a fast pace, momentum, not the muscle, is doing the majority of the work.

Form
The correct posture is essential for the prevention of injury. Always look in the mirror when you are lifting weights as it gives you the ability to see if

you are arching the back, leaning to one side or over balancing. If one side is stronger than the other, as you look in the mirror, you can make adjustments so as to even out the lift. I always recommend start weight lifting with barbells. It is much easier to keep this level and have balance with the movement. Dumbbells at the beginning can be difficult to maintain an even lift and should be used for the more advanced lifter.

It is **very** important to maintain a straight back when lifting. We have a tendency to arch the back as we lift, as it seems easier when trying to get the weight moved. This only adds to the pressure and stresses already on the back muscles. These muscles are usually the stabilising muscles, and it causes them to strain. Over time, this will injure your back and you will start to feel backache when you lift.

Weight

Using the correct weight is vital. More is not necessary better. If a weight is so heavy that you have to jerk, bounce or swing to get it to the top of the movement, **it's too heavy**. Your form will be compromised. It is better to start with a lighter weight so that you can master the movement first and then move on to the heavier weights. Be sensible - look at the other people in the gym who are straining - they are potential injury cases!

Sequence

When choosing which exercises to do it is best to start with the larger muscle groups and work toward the smaller muscle groups. This allows you to do the most demanding moves when you're the least fatigued. For example, you're less likely to lose your balance during a lunge if you do the lunges before tiring the muscles of the quads and hamstrings. Likewise you will have better form doing your push-ups if you do them before fatiguing the triceps with dips.

Knowing when enough is enough

I will talk about sets and reps further on but how many do I do, and, how do I know when I have done enough for me?

Start with one exercise per muscle group. Unless you are training to be the next world champion Body Builder, excessive training on one muscle group is unnecessary. You should have enough sets and reps to feel that the muscle has been worked, but not so much that you feel any burning! It should be just possible to finish the last rep without losing form. If you are straining and excessively grunting with the exertion, it is TOO much weight!!

Reps and Sets

A Rep is the number of times you repeat the exercise without resting.
The Set is a number of times you repeat that series.
For example if you were asked to do 4 sets of 10 tricep dips - it would be 10 triceps dips, rest for 90 seconds. Repeat and rest, and so on until you had completed 10 tricep dips, 4 times in total.
The amount of reps and sets depends on your goals.
To have higher reps and fewer sets will achieve muscle capacity i.e. the muscle becomes stronger.
To have the opposite such as fewer reps and more sets will achieve muscle resilience i.e. the muscle can perform for longer.
Obviously for the runner you have the two extremes. The sprinter wants more muscle mass to run faster whereas the long distance runner wants less muscle mass but more capacity so they can run further. The object is to balance the capacity with the resilience for maximum gains!

Progression

Progressive resistance is the key to any well planned strength training program. What this demonstrates is, as your muscle adapts to the given exercise, you can gradually increase the resistance or the repetitions to obtain further gains. There are several ways to achieve this.

The first method is to start with a weight that allows you to do at least 8 repetitions of that exercise. Once you can complete 12 repetitions with that weight, you increase the weight by about 5 percent. Now, you're doing 8 repetitions with the slightly heavier weight. Once you've worked up to 12 repetitions with the heavier weight, you increase it by another 5 percent (or no more than 10%) and go back to doing 8 repetitions. The idea is to keep alternately increasing repetitions and resistance, so that you continue to see results.

The second method is to start with a weight that allows you to do at least 8 repetitions of that exercise. Complete 4 sets of this exercise. Next week reduce to 3 sets and the week after reduce to 2 sets. Repeat this 3 week cycle and only increase the weight on the 3 set week by 5lbs or the smallest weight allowance. Maintain this weight until you are ready to increase again but only do so during the 3 set week.

I have only described two techniques but as you can see there are a variety of programs and procedures that can be followed. How to choose one over the other depends on your goals. For the middle distance runner I would recommend 8 to 10 reps and 3 to 4 sets depending on the week of your annual plan which I cover in my Teach Me: How to Run a 10K Faster book or Teach Me: Weight Training both due out soon.

How often should I do Weight Training?

The benefits of weight training such as the increases in muscle size and strength don't occur in the gym they happen during the rest period between workouts. This is when your muscles recover and rebuild, gradually becoming bigger and stronger. This recovery process takes at least 48 hours, as discussed in the Rest and Regeneration chapter. For this reason, weight training sessions should be scheduled no more frequently than every other day. Once or twice a week is ample. Arms and core one day, legs and core the other.

Sport specific exercises

Biceps
Bicep curls with barbell, dumbbells, or a machine.

Triceps
Tricep dips, on the machine, with dumbbells or using a bench.

Abdominals
Reverse crunches & curls, involving a rotation or twist.

TEACH ME: How to Run

Hip abductors and adductors
Side leg lifts while standing or lying.

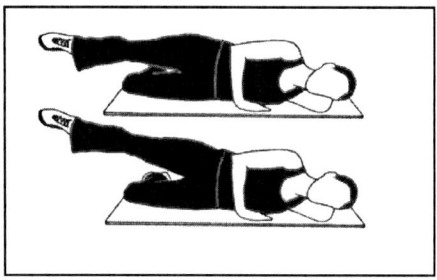

Quadriceps –
Lunges, leg extension machine, and leg press machine.

CHAPTER 8: Weight Training

Hamstrings
Squats, leg curl machine, lunges and leg press machine.

Calf
Calf raises seated, standing or using the Swiss Ball.

TEACH ME: How to Run

Chapter 9 – Race Day Preparations

How to choose the right race for you
The week before training guide
Race day preparations

Why run a race?

You run to test yourself, to prove all the training has been worth it!

When you race it's you alone who confronts the challenge of the race.

Racing appeals to millions of people and there are hundreds of races to choose from and attend. But which is the right one for you?

If you have never raced before then now is the time to give it a try.
All levels of runners race for a whole variety of reasons.

So, as the big day approaches what is the best preparation? Some people thrive on the competition whereas others find it all too overwhelming. Whichever you are, try and enjoy yourself and have a good time.

How to choose the right race for you

A good way to choose the race for you is to pick a race distance that is a third of your weekly mileage. Most importantly pick a distance that you think you can *complete* at this stage as opposed to *compete*! A good starting race is the 5K and there are plenty of those from Fun Runs to serious races. When you get more experience, then is the time for the longer distances.

- You must give yourself time to prepare for the race and don't think you can just run a 5K because you did it back in High School!
- Things to think about are the weather conditions – do you really like to run in the rain and wind? If not, then don't choose a race in February or March.
- Try not to plan a too rigid time goal. Run your first race for the fun of it and to enjoy the experience.
- Do you like crowds? If you are not one for big crowds then a huge race with thousands of people is not the race for you. They are great for motivating you on, if you like that, but a terrifying experience if you don't like being jostled or surrounded by people.
- If you drink lots of water, make sure that the race has water stations around the course.
- Do you want an accurate time? Choose a race with chip timers that record your time as you go over the line at the start and the finish, as opposed to when the gun goes off, to when you finish. If there are crowds of people it could take you 10 minutes to actually get to the start line to start the race!

The week before the race

You should be thinking about tapering your training so as to get enough recovery before the big day. If you follow the training guide for the 10K in chapter 2 it already includes a taper. For the beginners you will need to reduce your training starting 2 weeks before the race.

The general guide is to have 2 days before the race as total rest. For your last week start with a 30 minute run with 1 week to go. Then plan 2 runs during that week; a 20 minute run about 5 days before, and, your last run for 10 minutes 3 days before race day. Now is not the time to be starting new running routines or running long distances. The more you run in that last week, the slower you will be on race day. You need to run enough to keep your legs mobilized, but rest enough to be full of energy on race day!

Food
Now is not the time to be trying new recipes or new restaurants. You have worked hard to get to this stage and it would be dreadful to have to pull out of the race because of an upset stomach or food poisoning! Read the chapter 5 for food race day preparations.

Footwear
New shoes need at least a couple of week's braking in before a race.

Getting to the Race
Plan on how you are going to get there and where to park. If it is a large race with 1,000's of people remember there will be thousands of people trying to park near the event.

Go to get your Bib and Chip
If it's a large race your bib & chip will be available to pick up the day before otherwise with the smaller races, you can get them on the day.

TEACH ME: How to Run

Race Day

Before you leave
- Eat as you would normally do on any other training day or session. One hour beforehand have a small snack of protein and carbs. Not too much so it will sit in your stomach.
- Wear layers of clothes so you can take off during the race and tie round your waist. Be sure to have extra clothes to wear after the race - you will get cold even if it is a hot climate or in case it rains.
- Check your chip is on your shoe and you have your bib number.
- Prepare a protein shake to have for after the race, and a drink if there won't be any water provided at the event.

At the event
- Get there early, so you are relaxed and don't have to worry about parking miles away from the event.
- If you are meeting people find a location away from the start and is not too crowded.
- Don't wear new clothes, they can rub and cause bleeding.
- Don't wear new shoes!
- Washroom break, 20 minutes before the race. This allows for any queues and getting to the start line.
- Get to the start line in plenty of time. The gun may go off earlier than you think and starting from the back is not great!

At the start
- Do a Warm up. Walk around briskly for 15 minutes or gently jog. This will keep you warm and calm your excitement.
- Don't take off clothes until you have started running. Tie around your waist and have to put on when you finish. Better still get a friend to hand your clothes to, just before the start and give back to you at the end.

During the race
- DON'T get caught up in the excitement of the other runners and get carried along. PACE yourself FROM THE START. You know how fast you can run so don't use all your energy in the first half of the race.

- Try not to have too high expectations in your first race – use this as a starting point and so you can work from this.
- HAVE FUN!! Enjoy the atmosphere and the excitement of the race.
- Drink small amounts as you go round if there are water stops, if not drink at the end.
- Don't feel you have to finish the race if you are injured. If you are in pain - stop and assess. If it eases and you can carry on, take it easy for a while. If it hurts too much, don't try and be brave! Stop and call for medical help.

After the race
- COOL DOWN. Walk round for 10 minutes to flush out the muscles; it will reduce the DOMS the next day!
- Recovery is crucial. Make sure you eat and drink well after the race. Proteins and Carbs – a good breakfast at some café or restaurant is ideal.
- Don't get too cold. Put on clothes straight away and sweat in them so you don't get a chill.
- When you get home ice any aching muscles and relax!!

The week after
- Rest for at least a week afterwards and give your body time to recover.
- Use some of Therapeutic Modalities described in Chapter 6 - Rest and Recovery.

Now is the time to reflect on the race, it will tell you what you need to work on:
- I was too slow – more speed work is needed.
- I ran out of energy half way round – either you ran off too fast or you haven't built enough capacity yet. You will need to work on distance.
- I didn't enjoy the experience – racing is just not for you!!

If you want to know what to do next, time to buy one of my other books in the Teach Me series that will be published soon.

Check out my website: www.redboxbooks.org

Glossary of Terms

Adaptation
Changes experienced in the individual after different stimuli have been introduced.

Aerobic
A reaction or motion that occurs that requires oxygen.

Aerobic Capacity
Total amount of energy that can be produced aerobically by an individual.

Aerobic Endurance
Ability to sustain a sub-maximal power output over time through aerobic energy production.

Agility
A term that describes motor patterns characterized by a high degree of motor control, coordination and speed.

Anaerobic
A reaction or motion that occurs, without requiring oxygen.

Anaerobic Capacity
Total amount of energy that can be produced without using oxygen by an individual. This is usually determined by all out effort from 45 - 90 seconds.

Balance
The ability to maintain a relative level of equilibrium by means of an appropriate position and make use of compensatory movements.

Cool Down
Procedure that progressively reduces the metabolic rate transitioning the tissues from work to rest. This is generally recognized as being the first stage of any recovery strategy.

Coordination
The synchronization of different muscles which allows an individual to execute more or less complex movements in the correct sequence.

Endurance
The ability to sustain a given power output over time.

Energy
The capacity to do work.

Exercise
General term that refers to the repeated execution of actions, skills or movements for the improvement of physical abilities.

Fatigue
The point at which power output can no longer be sustained.

Fitness
The general term that describes the capability of an individual to handle the requirements of a specific physical, mental, cognitive or motor task.

Flexibility
The ability to conduct movements in certain joints with an appropriate range of motion.

Goal Setting
The mental representation of a performance to be accomplished, and the steps leading to this performance.

Intensity
The tension generated or the power output developed during an exercise.

Interval Training
Training method in which periods of effort and recovery of various durations are systematically alternated to obtain different training effects.

GLOSSARY OF TERMS

Mobilization
Moving the limbs to lubricate the joints.

Recovery
The process of restoring physical and or mental work capacities following effort or fatigue.

Relaxation
A mental preparation technique used to relieve excessive stress.

Speed
The ability to react to a stimulus or signal in the shortest possible time.

Super-compensation
State of increased work capacity to tolerate training above the level recently attainable.

Tapering Procedure
Training procedure used in the weeks leading up to a race which is aimed at enhancing the super-compensation effect and enabling the athlete to reach peak performance.

Training Program
Description and prescription of the various methods employed to achieve specific performance objectives.

Training Session
A specific period of time set aside for the systematic and organised development or maintenance of performance factors.

Warm Up
Procedure that progressively increases the metabolic rate preparing the tissues for work from rest.

TEACH ME: How to Run

Bibliography

References from:

Injury Prevention
Fred Lebow – Complete book of Running and Fitness
Wynn Gmitroski - Athlete Injury Prevention
Tim Noakes – Lore of Running

Stretching and Flexibility
Brad Appleton – Stretching and Flexibility
Kathleen B. Williamson, M.S., R.N., C, Coordinator of Cardiopulmonary Fitness Program
Sport Stretch, by Michael J. Alter

Nutrition
J. Hawley and L. Burke. Sydney: Allen & Unwin, 1998
Patricia Chuey – The 101 most asked Nutrition Questions

Rest and Recovery
Dave Spence - Time-to-Run article
Wynn Gmitroski – Rest and Recovery

Core Stability
Core Stability – Peak Performance article
Pilates Institute – London
Paige Waehner - PlusOneActive

Weight Training
Art Liberman – Marathon Training
Renee Cloe – Strength Training Basics